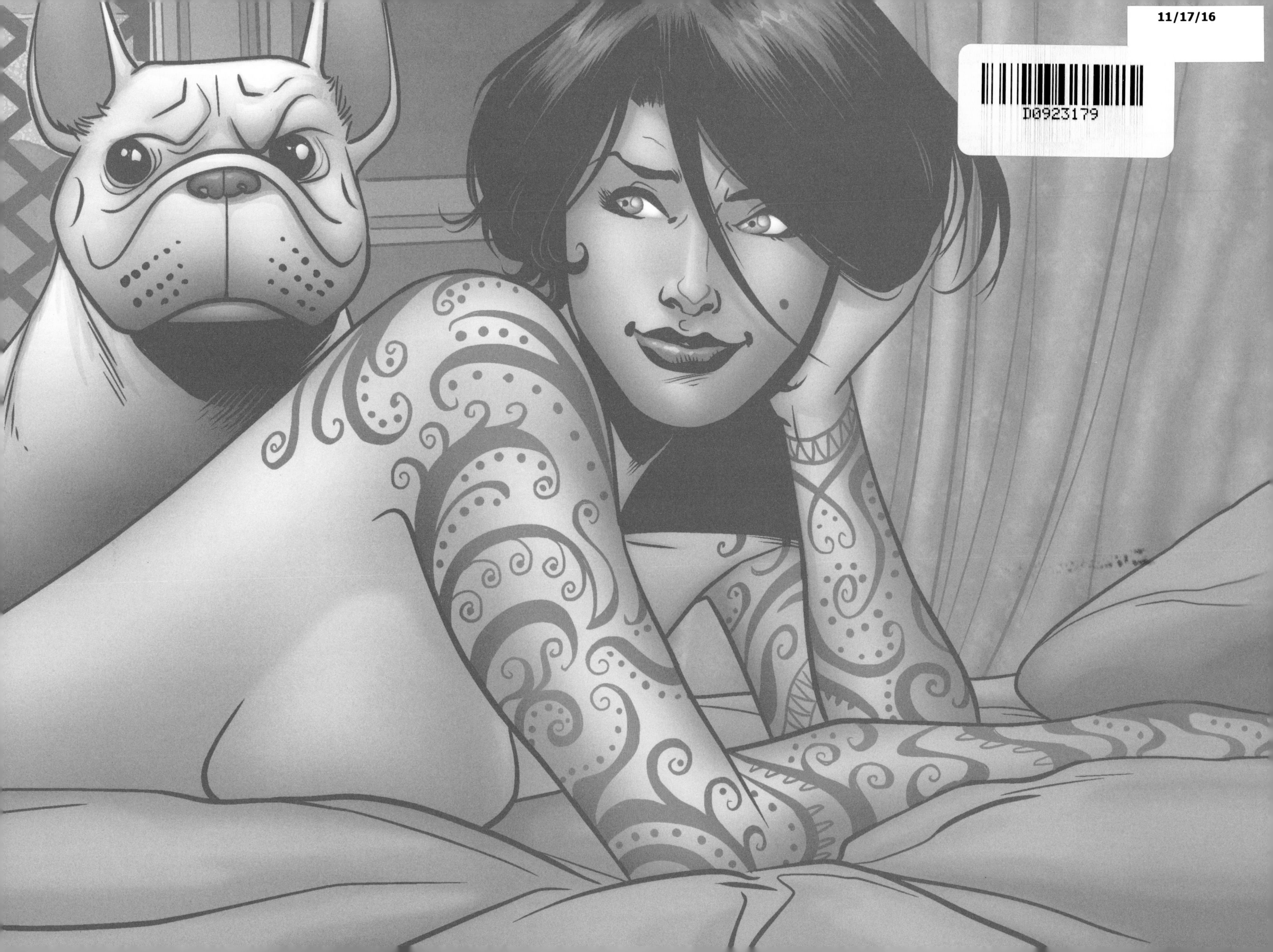

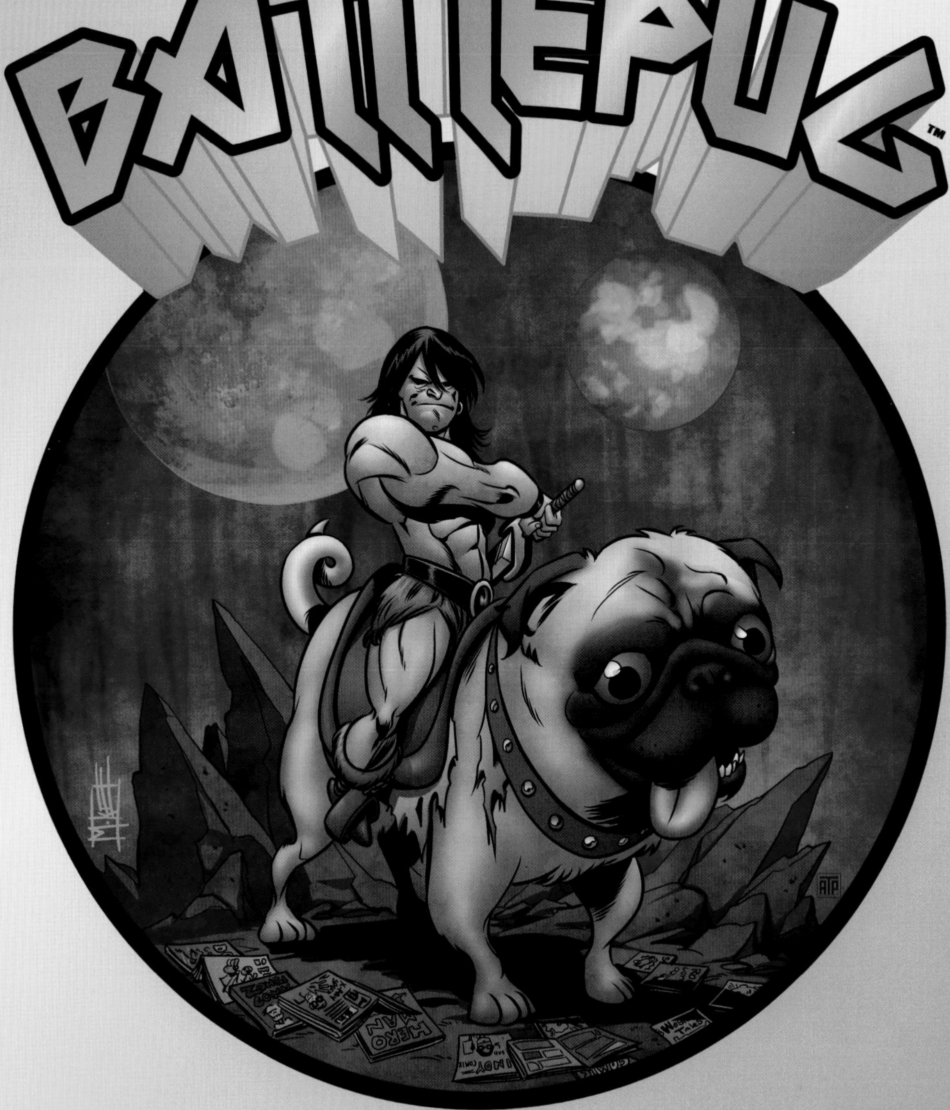
BATTLEPUG™

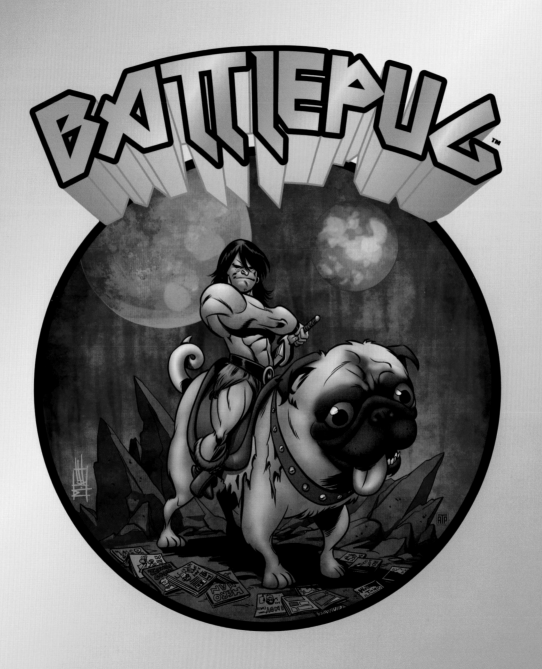

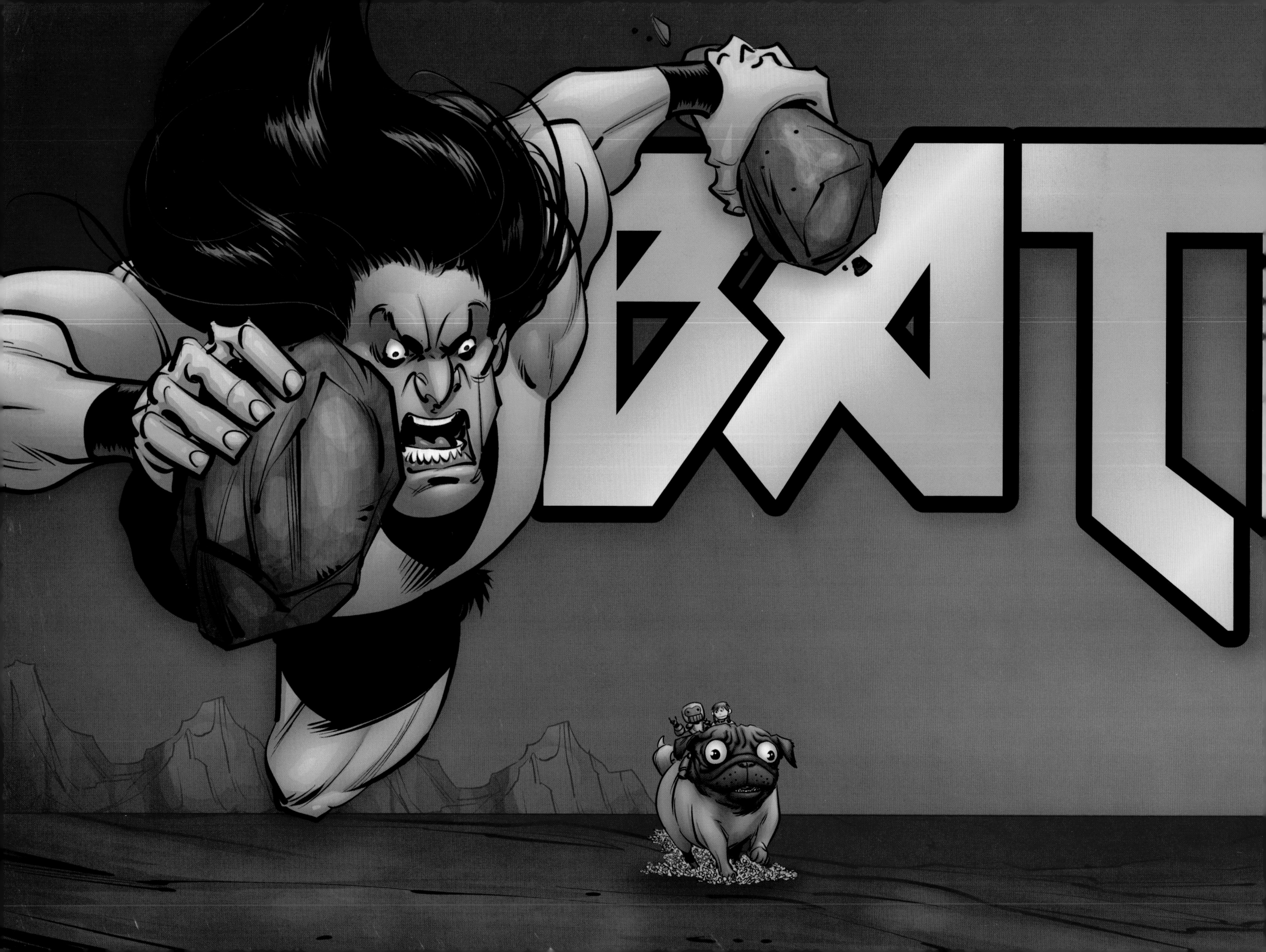

VOLUME 5: THE PAWS OF WAR

BATTLEPUG ™

Writer and Artist
MIKE NORTON

Color Artist
ALLEN PASSALAQUA

Letterer
CHRIS CRANK

Cover Artists
MIKE NORTON AND
ALLEN PASSALAQUA

DARK HORSE
BOOKS

President and Publisher
MIKE RICHARDSON

Editor
PATRICK THORPE

Assistant Editor
CARDNER CLARK

Designer
TINA ALESSI

Digital Art Technician
CHRISTIANNE GOUDREAU

Published by Dark Horse Books, a division of Dark Horse Comics, Inc.
10956 SE Main Street, Milwaukie, Oregon 97222
DarkHorse.com | Facebook.com/DarkHorseComics | Twitter.com/DarkHorseComics

To find a comic shop in your area, call the Comic Shop Locator Service: (888) 266-4226

First edition: October 2016
ISBN 978-1-50670-114-1
10 9 8 7 6 5 4 3 2 1
Printed in China

Library of Congress Cataloging-in-Publication Data

Names: Norton, Mike, 1949- writer and artist. | Passalaqua, Allen, color artist.
Title: Battlepug Volume 5 / by Mike Norton.
Description: First edition. | Milwaukie, OR : Dark Horse Books, 2016.
Identifiers: LCCN 2015289021 | ISBN 9781506701141
Subjects: LCSH: Graphic novels. | Pug comic books, strips, etc.
Classification: LCC PN6727.N67 B38 2012 | DDC 741.5/973--dc23
LC record available at http://lccn.loc.gov/2015289021

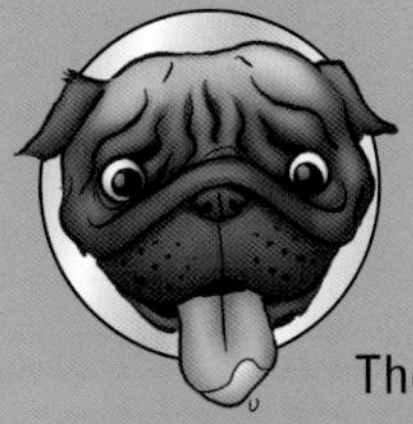

IN WHICH WE BID *BATTLEPUG* A LONG AND BUTTERY FAREWELL

In the remote and lofty reaches of Tibet, monks sculpt elaborate multicolored statues of the Buddha out of pigmented butter. They're painstaking in their work, which is a combination of art and sacred devotion. After days and sometimes weeks of effort, when a given statue is done, in all of its exacting detail, refined and imposing, the monks let it rot. It slowly goes rancid, filling their temples, retreats, and monasteries with the stench of its decay, because—*y'know*—butter.

They do it to remind themselves of the inescapable law of transience. No matter what, all things must pass. Everything is ultimately doomed, and for some reason I can only occasionally begin to fathom, those recondite monks find this to be a cause for recurring celebration.

This, so I am told, is the fifth and final collection of Mike Norton's splendid *Battlepug*, because it's time, because all stories with such great beginnings and middles should eventually (perhaps even reluctantly) come to a satisfying end.

Because all things must pass.

But before the end, before you launch yourself into these wonderful final pages (assuming you're among the few who read introductions before the story, or even read introductions at all), let's spend a line or two talking about that beginning and middle.

It shouldn't have worked. I've a low tolerance for farce, that bastard defective offspring of comedy, because I live for a good story, and farce isn't overly concerned with building a coherent story, much less a good one. In fact the story parts of a farce exist solely to string together the manifest silly bits into just enough of a rudimentary chronology to get us from one nonsensical moment to the next. If the story grabs too much attention, the farce doesn't work as well. Sure, there have been some great works of farce. The entire oeuvre of Douglas Adams comes to mind. No one's done it better. In very small doses I enjoy his work as much as anyone. He was an unquestioned genius. But too much of any given one of his yarns at one reading and the unreality piles up, too deep to withstand. I need a story that matters, that can pull me into it, make me care about the characters and what happens to them, and fully engage me in whatever fictional consequences the author sets before us. Comedy or tragedy, that's what I absolutely must have from a story, and farce doesn't provide. It only exists to get us to the next silly bit, and then the one after that.

That's the reason I was fully prepared to dislike *Battlepug*. Sure, the art was gorgeous, but the parts seemed—well, let's be nice and call them "iffy." It was assembled from the components of farce. A barbarian warrior riding on a giant pug? Silly. A giant, cute monster baby seal, eventually killed with a candy cane? Cute, but silly. Evil Santa as a slave lord? Even more with the silly.

You probably know where I'm going with this. I read the first *Battlepug* collection reluctantly, because it was purchased for me as a gift, because it was created by an artist I admired (and I have to confess I was curious about his ability to write), and because it was so well drawn.

And I'll be damned, but the story drew me in. Almost against my will, calling Mike Norton's bluff, he engaged me. And it held me for four delightful collections. Now I need to know what happens to the barbarian without a name and his giant pug. I care about the fate of the daft old "Scribbly-Scrabbly" duffer, and the warrior woman, and the foulmouthed little girl. Somehow Mike took all of those elements that are impossible to combine into anything but slapstick, burlesque, and absurdity, and built a serious story out of them. No, not serious in the sense that nothing silly ever happens. People who confuse serious with the need to be relentlessly grim don't produce surprising works of art like *Battlepug*. For their sins, and lack of imagination, they become high-placed editors and movie moguls. *Battlepug* is a serious story because, even with all the funny bits, it requires us to care, and engage, and worry about how it all comes out.

As of this writing, I've no idea how it all comes out. Though I've read all four collections preceding this one, I've yet to read the pages contained here. They sent them to me so that I could write this opening note with some authority, but I decided instead to write about the sense of anticipation I feel, as I'm about to find out how it ends. I've invested a lot so far, because the story is just that good. I'll be surprised if he doesn't stick the landing. We'll see.

In fact, right now, let's all go see how it ends.

BILL WILLINGHAM
May 2, 2016

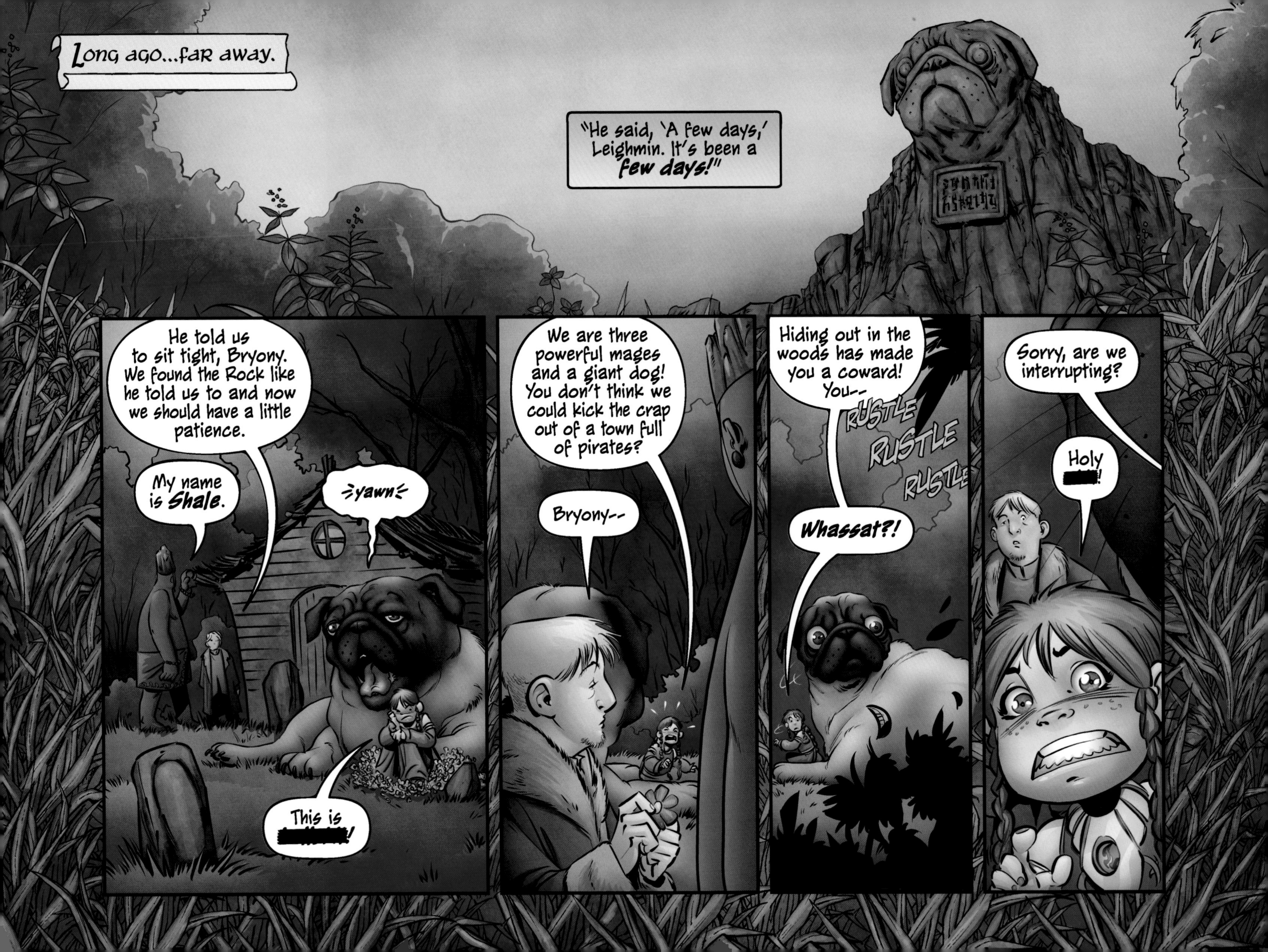
Long ago...far away.
"He said, 'A few days,' Leighmin. It's been a few days!"
He told us to sit tight, Bryony. We found the Rock like he told us to and now we should have a little patience.
My name is Shale.
≈yawn≈
This is [redacted]!
We are three powerful mages and a giant dog! You don't think we could kick the crap out of a town full of pirates?
Bryony--
Hiding out in the woods has made you a coward! You--
RUSTLE RUSTLE RUSTLE
Whassat?!
Sorry, are we interrupting?
Holy [redacted]!

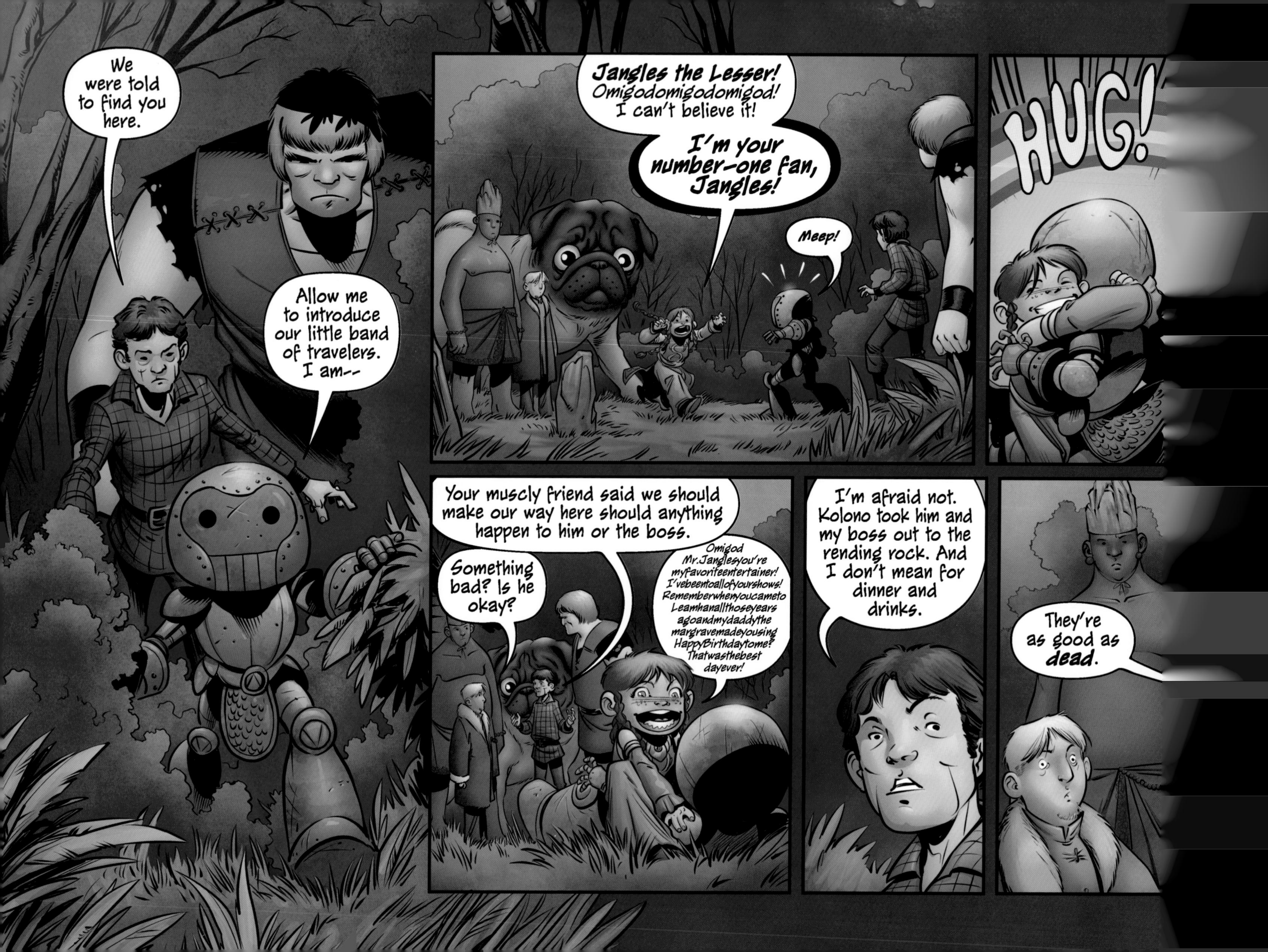

We were told to find you here.
Allow me to introduce our little band of travelers. I am--
Jangles the Lesser! Omigodomigodomigod! I can't believe it!
I'm your number-one fan, Jangles!
Meep!
HUG!
Your muscly friend said we should make our way here should anything happen to him or the boss.
Something bad? Is he okay?
Omigod Mr.Janglesyou're myfavoriteentertainer! I'vebeentoallofyourshows! Rememberwhenyoucameto Leamhanallthoseyears agoandmydaddythe margravemadeyousing HappyBirthdaytome? Thatwasthebest dayever!
I'm afraid not. Kolono took him and my boss out to the rending rock. And I don't mean for dinner and drinks.
They're as good as dead.

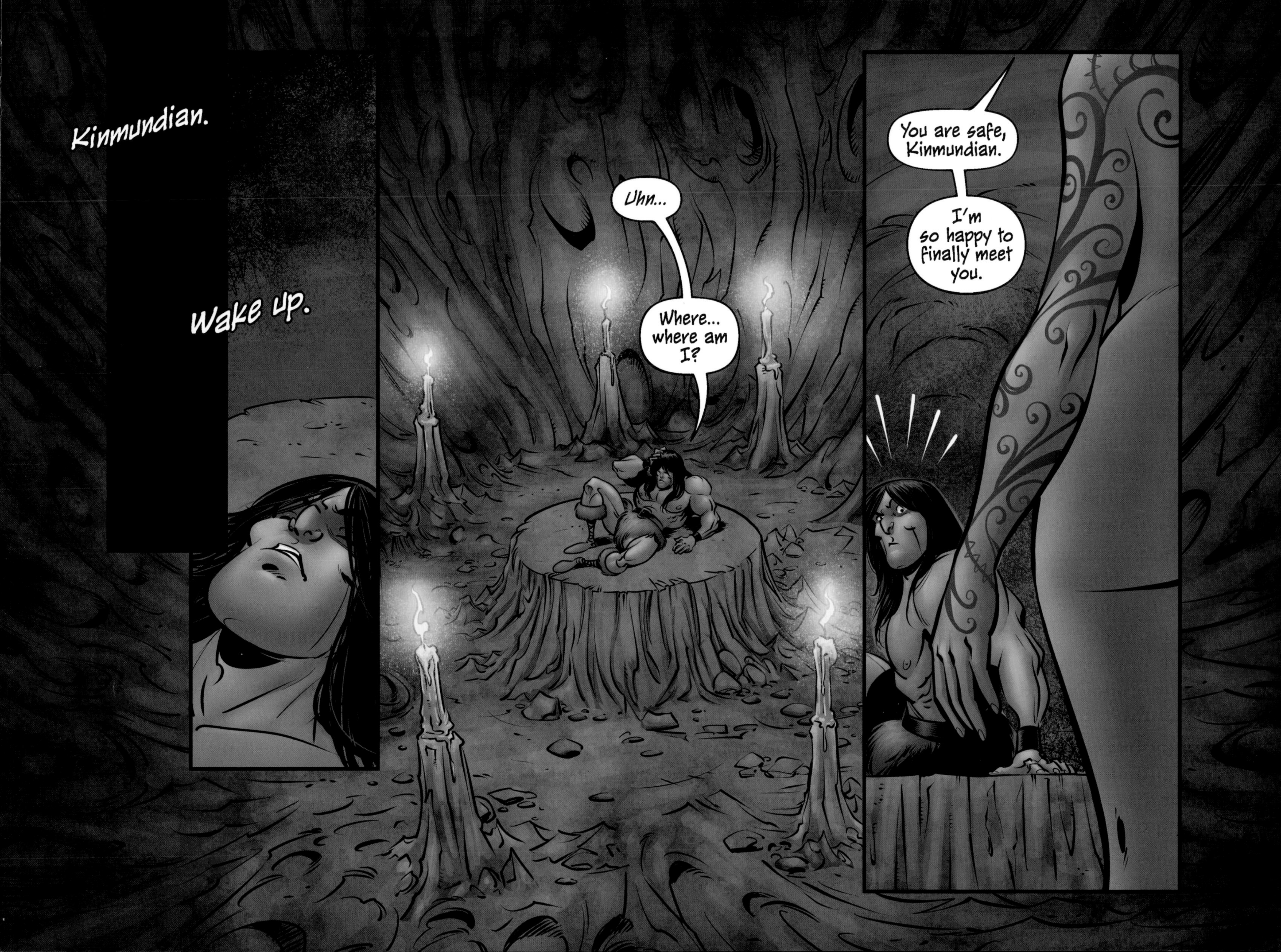
Kinmundian.
Wake up.
Uhn...
Where... where am I?
You are safe, Kinmundian.
I'm so happy to finally meet you.

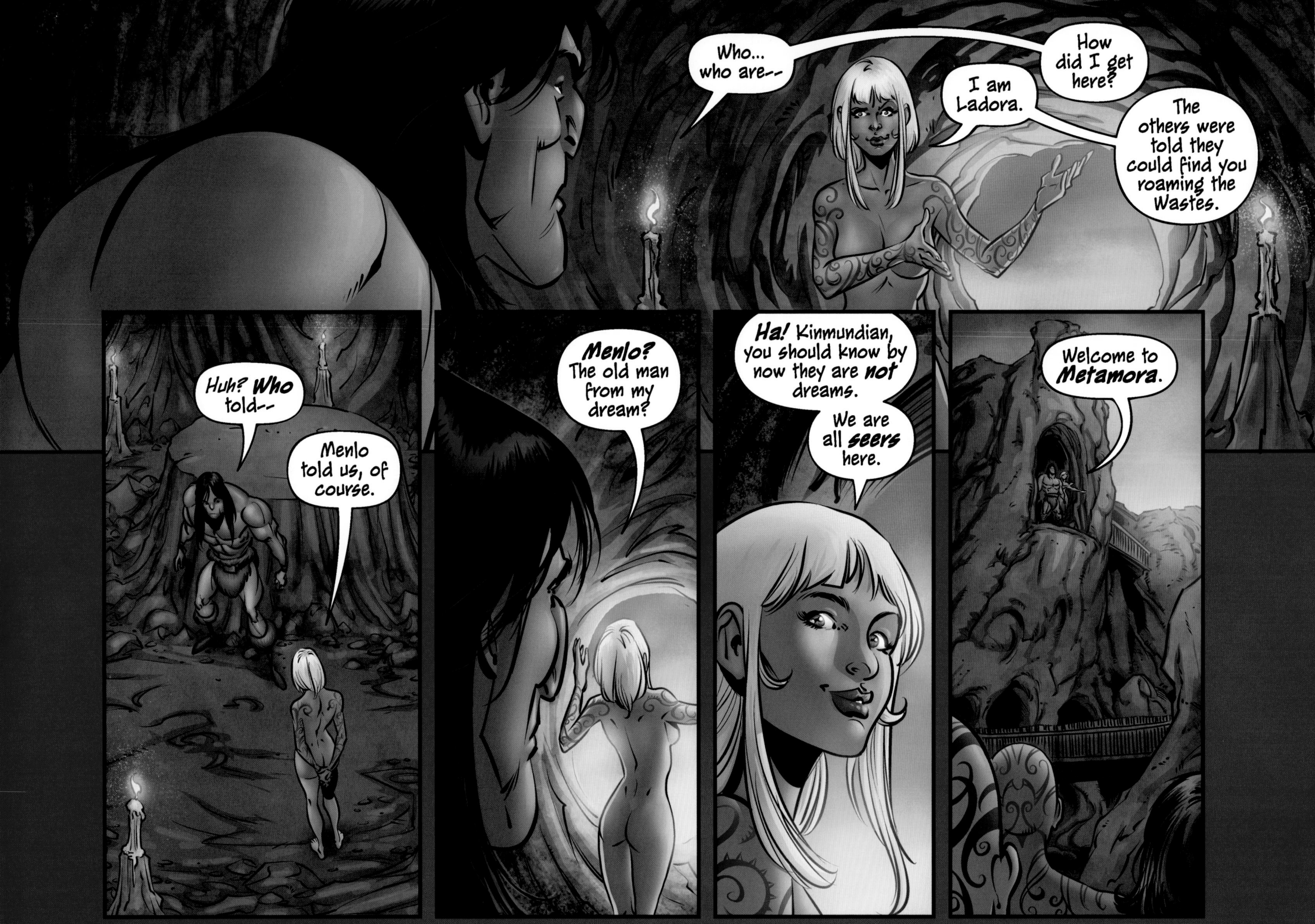
Who...
who are--
How did I get here?
I am Ladora.
The others were told they could find you roaming the Wastes.
Huh? Who told--
Menlo told us, of course.
Menlo? The old man from my dream?
Ha! Kinmundian, you should know by now they are not dreams.
We are all seers here.
Welcome to Metamora.

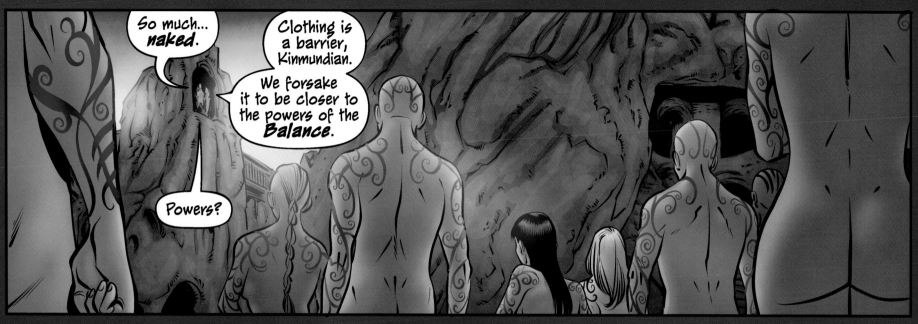

So much... *naked*.

Clothing is a barrier, Kinmundian. We forsake it to be closer to the powers of the *Balance*.

Powers?

You mages can command animal, vegetable, and mineral. We have our *own* gifts.

Allowing us to be better guides for those we are bonded with.

Some of us can speak through our minds, see the future, or see events far away as if we were there.

For everything else, we have our *seeing pool*. Would you like to visit--

No. I've *experienced* it before.

It's how we found the both of you in the Wastes.

Both?

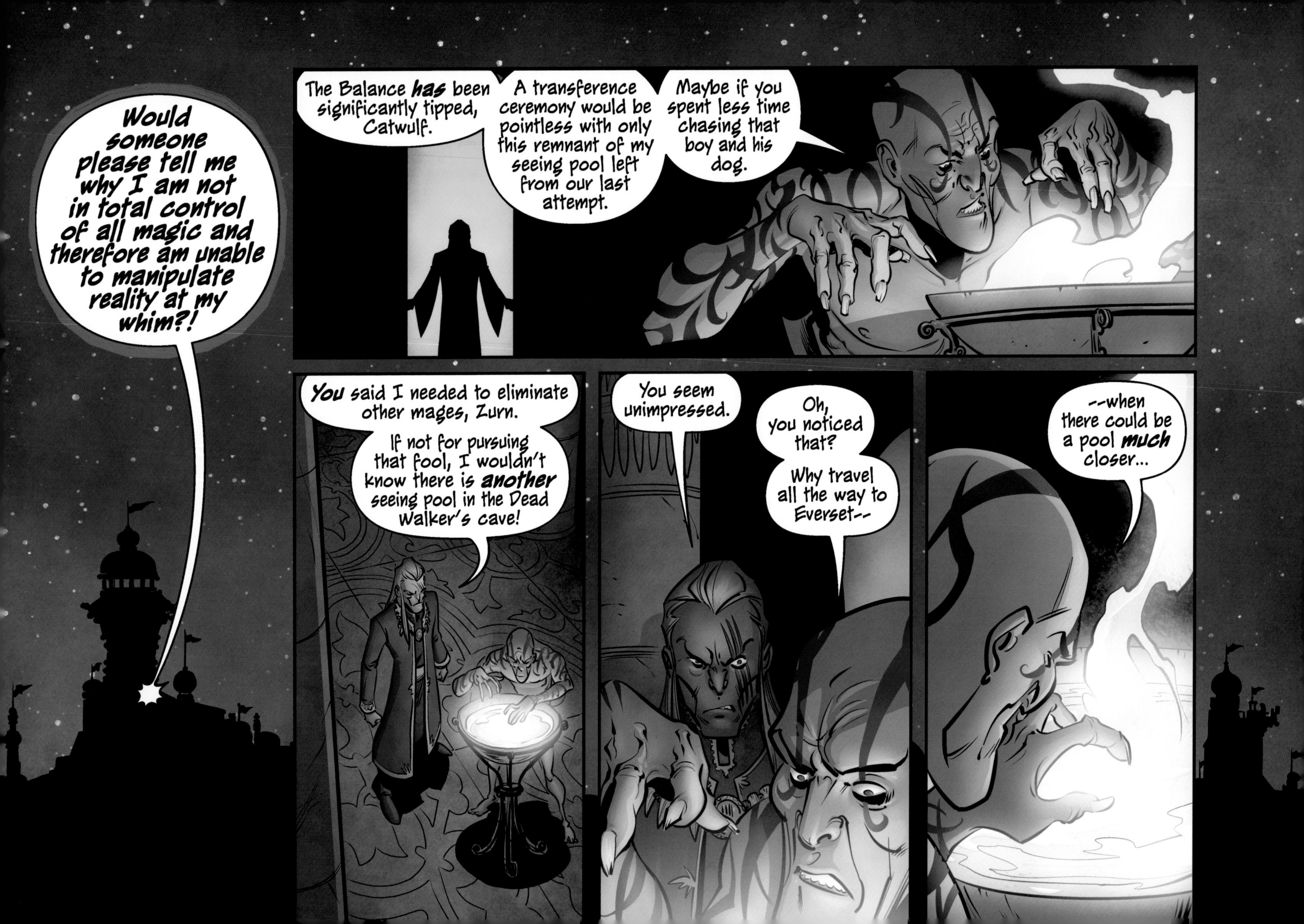
Would someone please tell me why I am not in total control of all magic and therefore am unable to manipulate reality at my whim?!
The Balance **has** been significantly tipped, Catwulf.
A transference ceremony would be pointless with only this remnant of my seeing pool left from our last attempt.
Maybe if you spent less time chasing that boy and his dog.
You said I needed to eliminate other mages, Zurn.
If not for pursuing that fool, I wouldn't know there is **another** seeing pool in the Dead Walker's cave!
You seem unimpressed.
Oh, you noticed that?
Why travel all the way to Everset--
--when there could be a pool **much** closer...

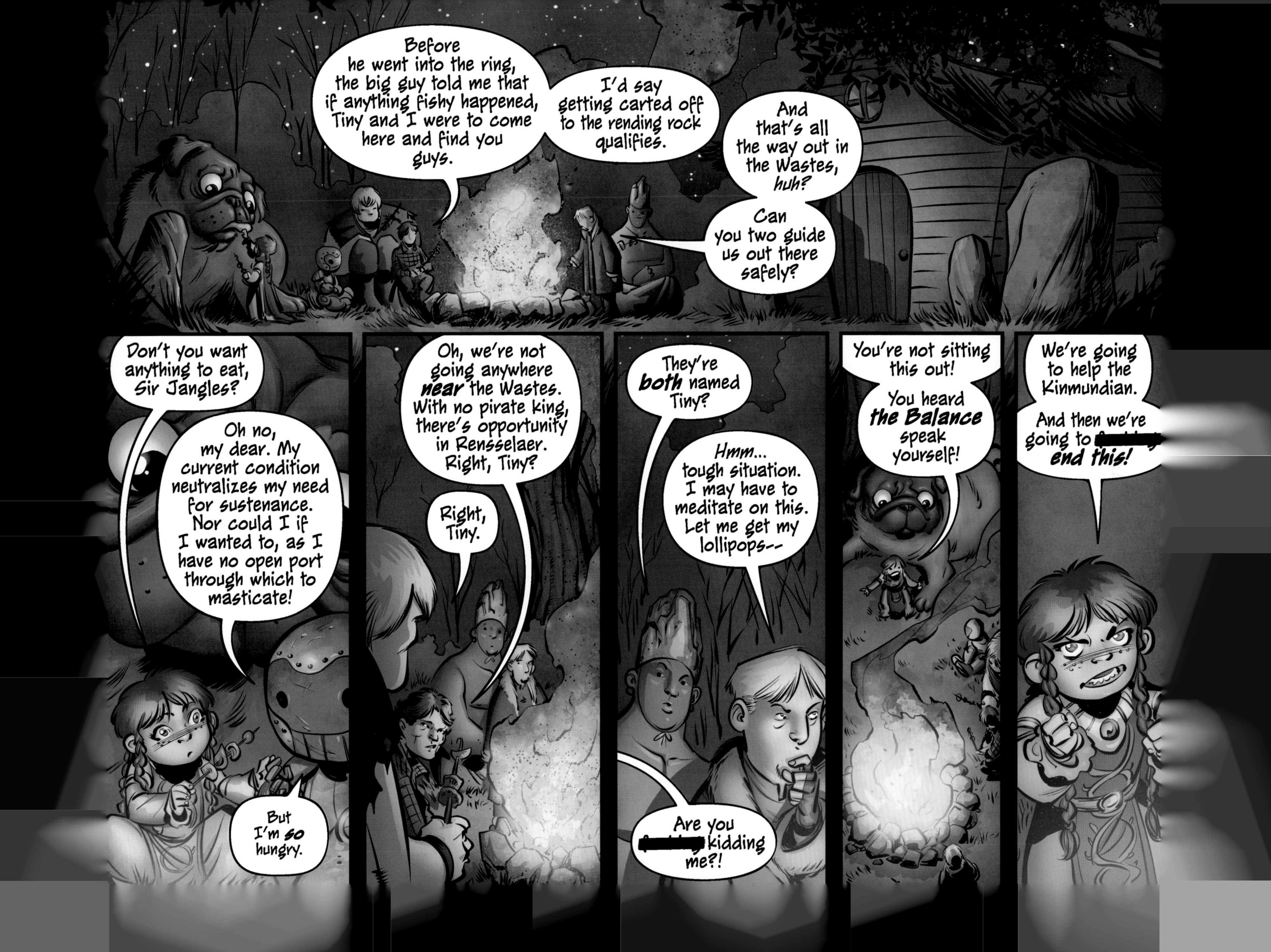

Before he went into the ring, the big guy told me that if anything fishy happened, Tiny and I were to come here and find you guys.
I'd say getting carted off to the rending rock qualifies.
And that's all the way out in the Wastes, *huh?*
Can you two guide us out there safely?
Don't you want anything to eat, Sir Jangles?
Oh no, my dear. My current condition neutralizes my need for sustenance. Nor could I if I wanted to, as I have no open port through which to masticate!
But I'm *so* hungry.
Oh, we're not going anywhere ***near*** the Wastes. With no pirate king, there's opportunity in Rensselaer. Right, Tiny?
Right, Tiny.
They're ***both*** named Tiny?
Hmm... tough situation. I may have to meditate on this. Let me get my lollipops--
Are you [redacted] kidding me?!
You're not sitting this out!
You heard ***the Balance*** speak yourself!
We're going to help the Kinmundian.
And then we're going to [redacted] ***end this!***

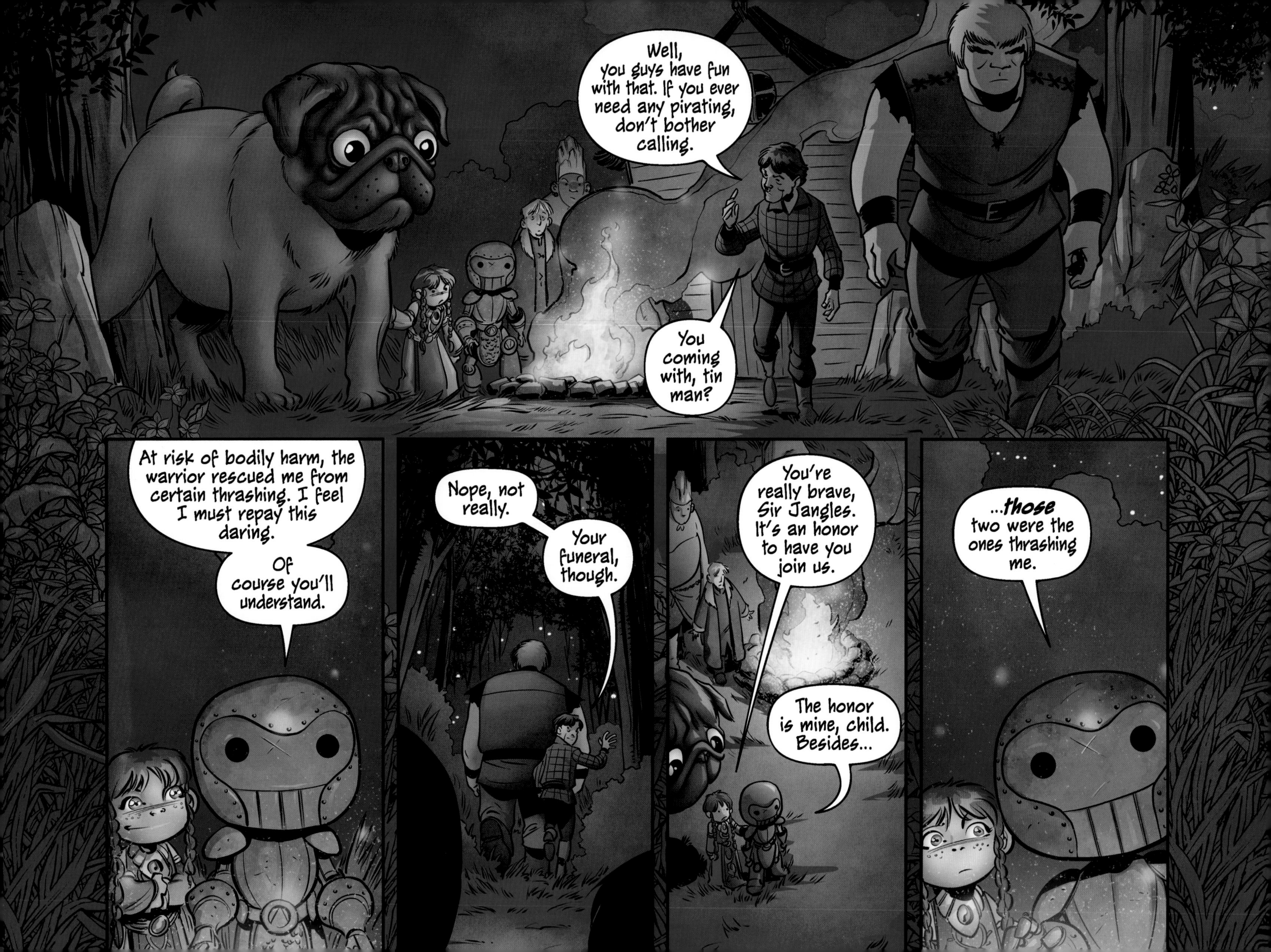
Well, you guys have fun with that. If you ever need any pirating, don't bother calling.
You coming with, tin man?
At risk of bodily harm, the warrior rescued me from certain thrashing. I feel I must repay this daring.
Of course you'll understand.
Nope, not really.
Your funeral, though.
You're really brave, Sir Jangles. It's an honor to have you join us.
The honor is mine, child. Besides...
...*those* two were the ones thrashing me.

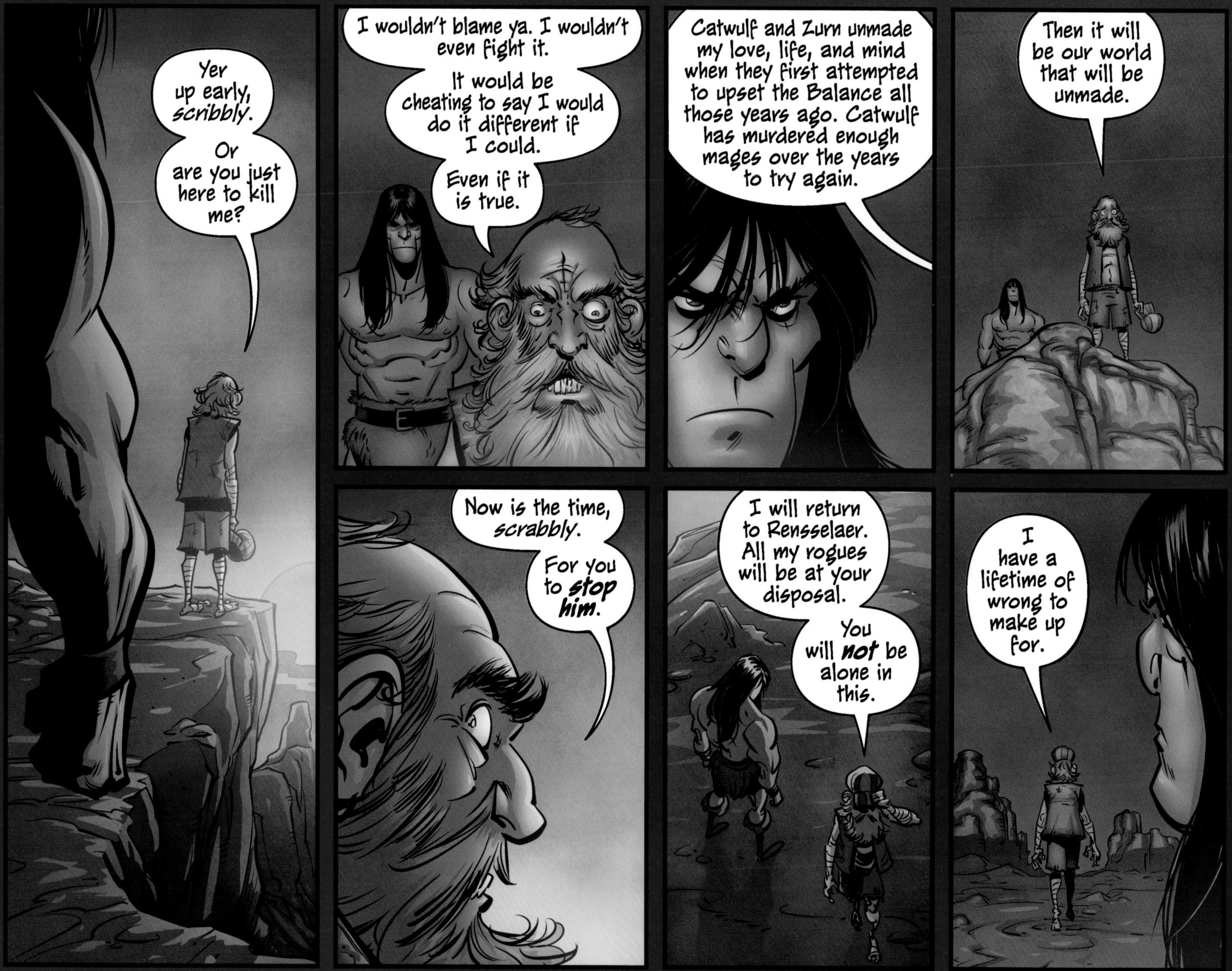
Yer up early, *scribbly*.
Or are you just here to kill me?
I wouldn't blame ya. I wouldn't even fight it.
It would be cheating to say I would do it different if I could.
Even if it is true.
Catwulf and Zurn unmade my love, life, and mind when they first attempted to upset the Balance all those years ago. Catwulf has murdered enough mages over the years to try again.
Then it will be our world that will be unmade.
Now is the time, *scrabbly*.
For you to ***stop him***.
I will return to Rensselaer. All my rogues will be at your disposal.
You will ***not*** be alone in this.
I have a lifetime of wrong to make up for.

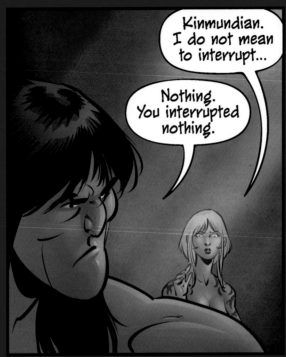
Kinmundian. I do not mean to interrupt...

Nothing. You interrupted nothing.

Of course. I have news from Menlo.

Menlo? But...

He would like to speak to you.

He spoke to me during the night. The rest of the seers heard it too.

But I'm not a *seer*. How am I supposed to--

Oh.

I *really* hate these things.

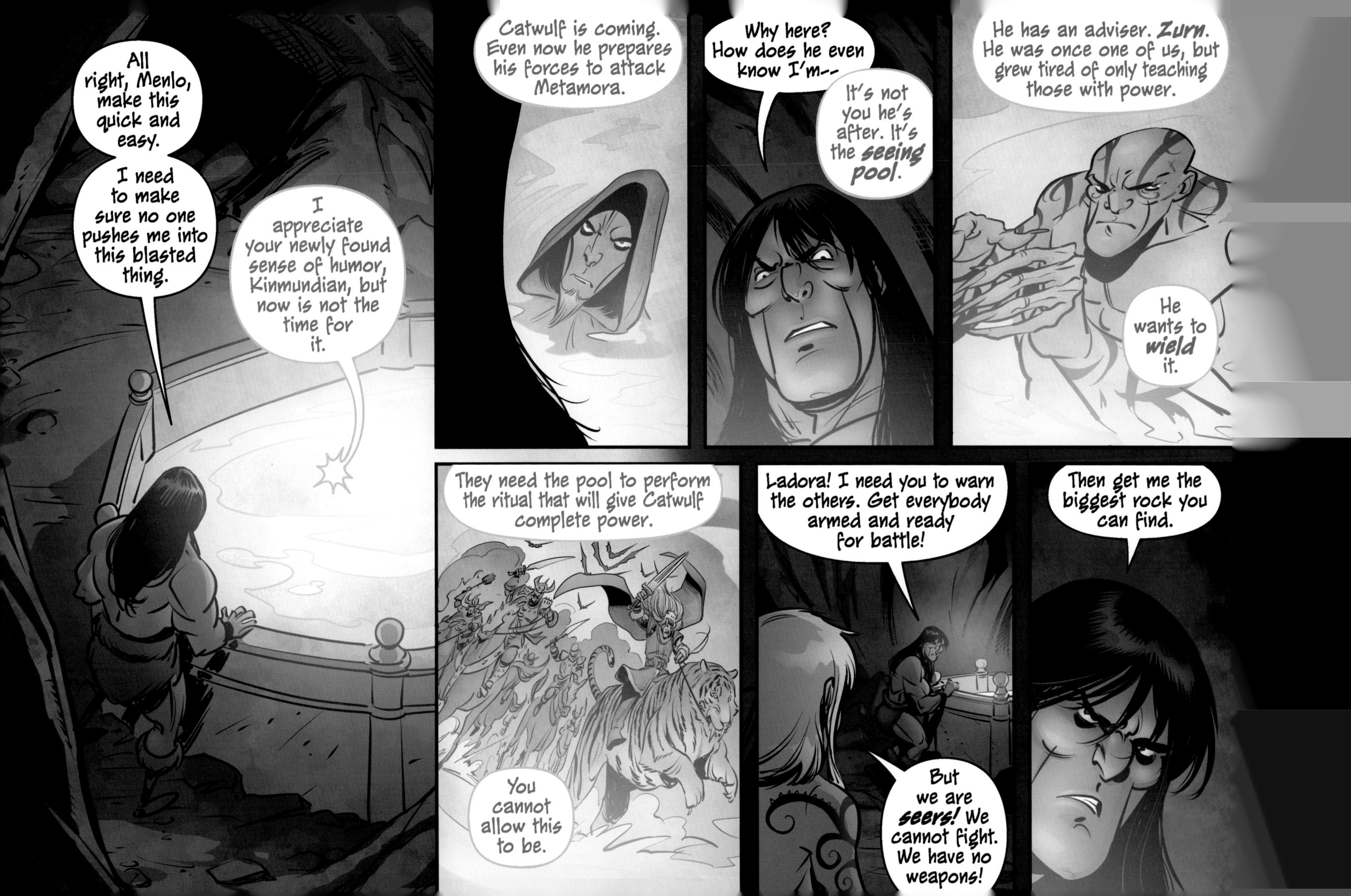
All right, Menlo, make this quick and easy.
I need to make sure no one pushes me into this blasted thing.
I appreciate your newly found sense of humor, Kinmundian, but now is not the time for it.
Catwulf is coming. Even now he prepares his forces to attack Metamora.
Why here? How does he even know I'm--
It's not you he's after. It's the seeing pool.
He has an adviser. Zurn. He was once one of us, but grew tired of only teaching those with power.
He wants to wield it.
They need the pool to perform the ritual that will give Catwulf complete power.
You cannot allow this to be.
Ladora! I need you to warn the others. Get everybody armed and ready for battle!
But we are seers! We cannot fight. We have no weapons!
Then get me the biggest rock you can find.

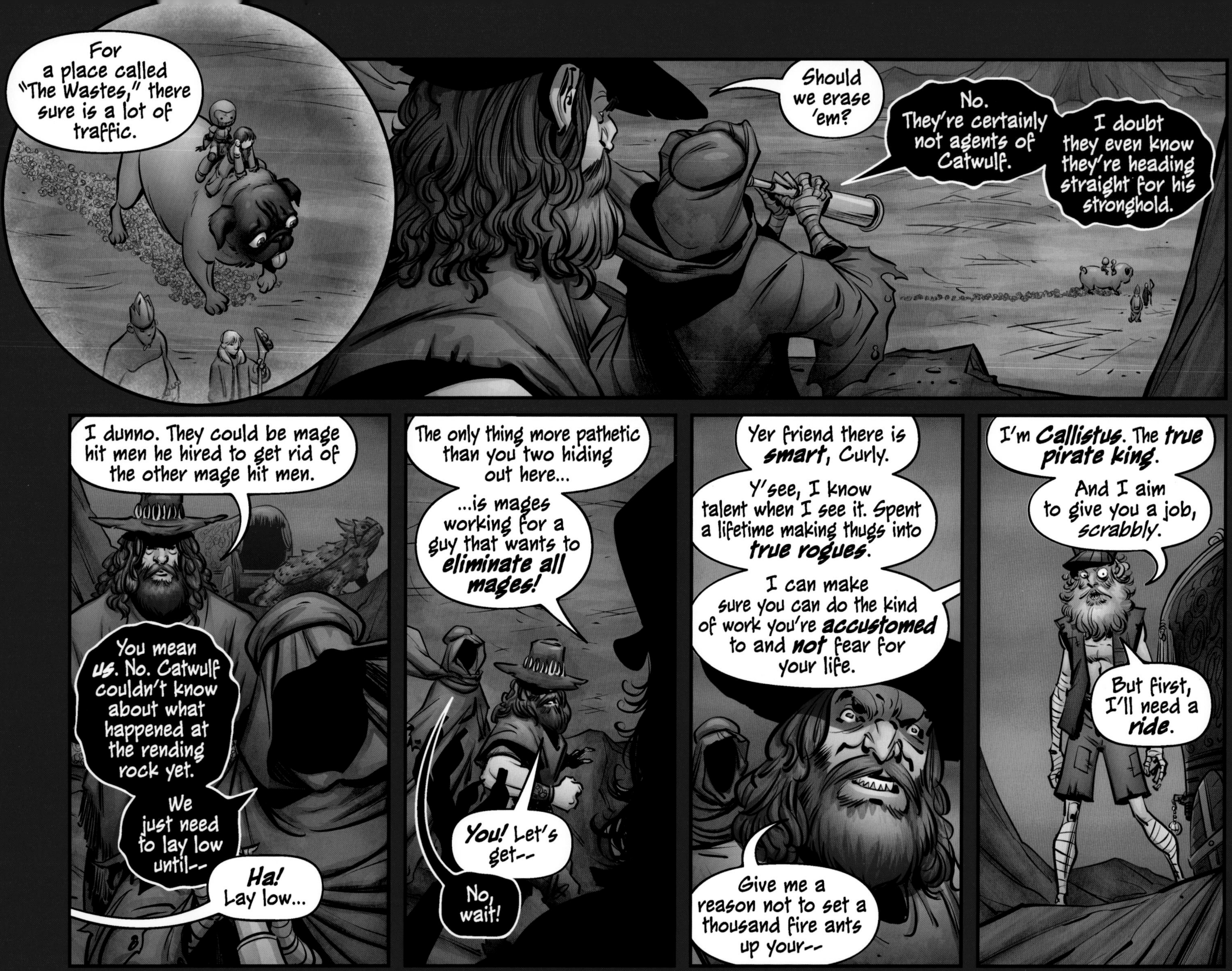

For a place called "The Wastes," there sure is a lot of traffic.
Should we erase 'em?
No. They're certainly not agents of Catwulf.
I doubt they even know they're heading straight for his stronghold.
I dunno. They could be mage hit men he hired to get rid of the other mage hit men.
You mean us. No. Catwulf couldn't know about what happened at the rending rock yet.
We just need to lay low until--
Ha! Lay low...
The only thing more pathetic than you two hiding out here...
...is mages working for a guy that wants to eliminate all mages!
You! Let's get--
No, wait!
Yer friend there is smart, Curly.
Y'see, I know talent when I see it. Spent a lifetime making thugs into true rogues.
I can make sure you can do the kind of work you're accustomed to and not fear for your life.
Give me a reason not to set a thousand fire ants up your--
I'm Callistus. The true pirate king.
And I aim to give you a job, scrabbly.
But first, I'll need a ride.

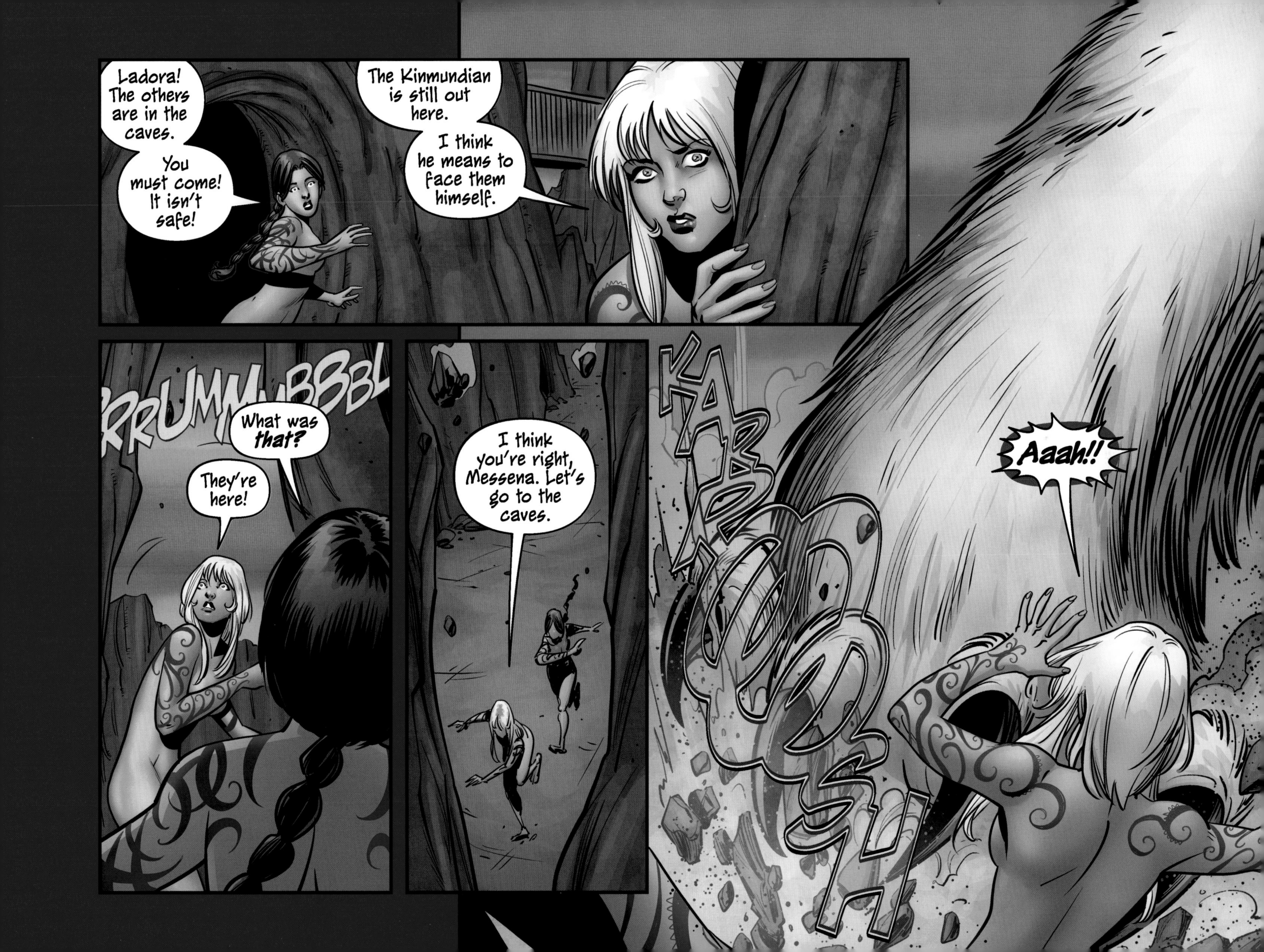
Ladora! The others are in the caves.
You must come! It isn't safe!
The Kinmundian is still out here.
I think he means to face them himself.
RRUMMMBBBL
What was *that?*
They're here!
I think you're right, Messena. Let's go to the caves.
KABOOOOSSH
Aaah!!

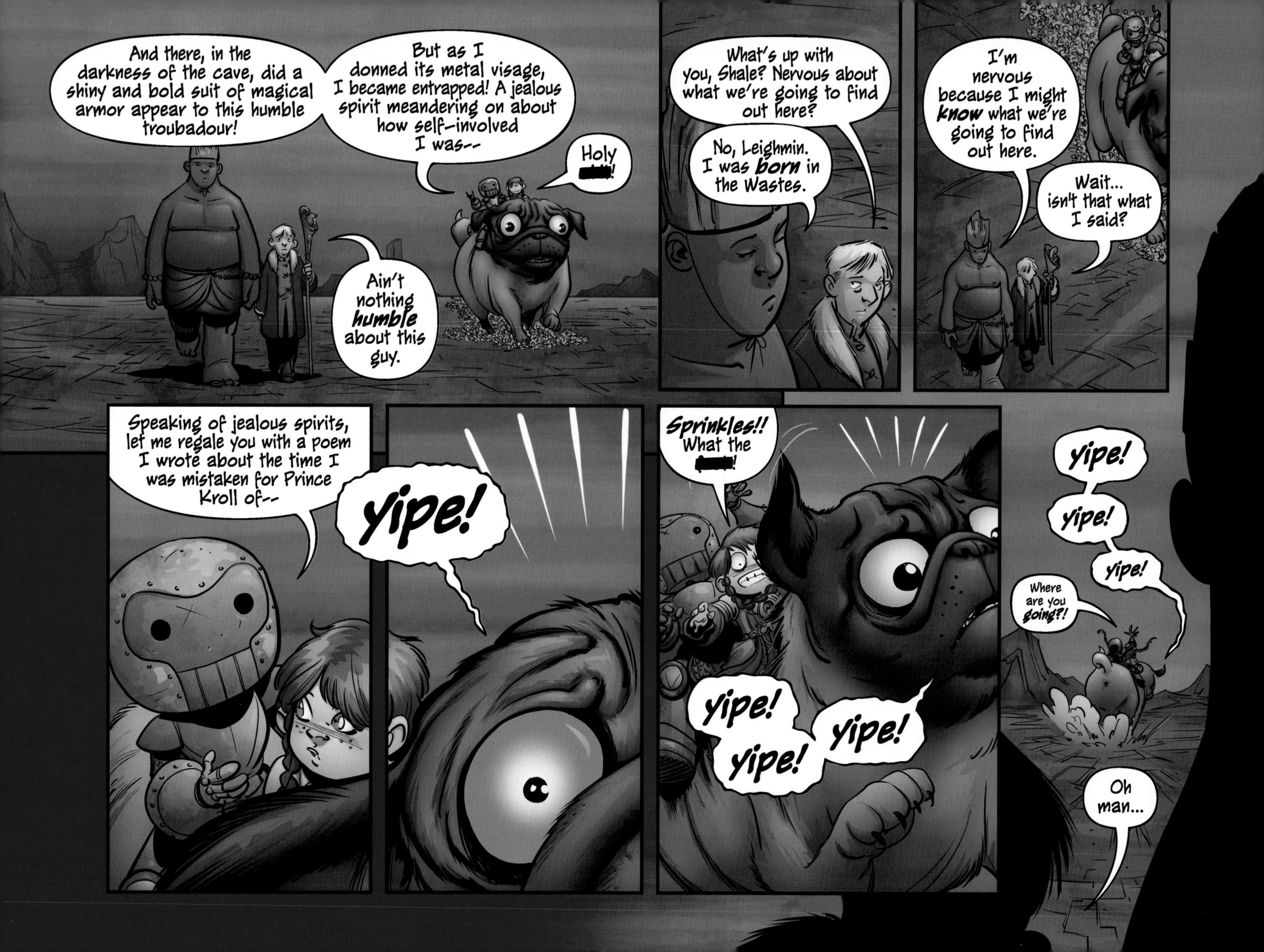

And there, in the darkness of the cave, did a shiny and bold suit of magical armor appear to this humble troubadour!
But as I donned its metal visage, I became entrapped! A jealous spirit meandering on about how self-involved I was--
Holy [redacted]!
Ain't nothing *humble* about this guy.
What's up with you, Shale? Nervous about what we're going to find out here?
No, Leighmin. I was *born* in the Wastes.
I'm nervous because I might *know* what we're going to find out here.
Wait... isn't that what I said?
Speaking of jealous spirits, let me regale you with a poem I wrote about the time I was mistaken for Prince Kroll of--
yipe!
Sprinkles!! What the [redacted]!
yipe!
yipe!
yipe!
yipe!
yipe!
yipe!
Where are you *going?!*
Oh man...

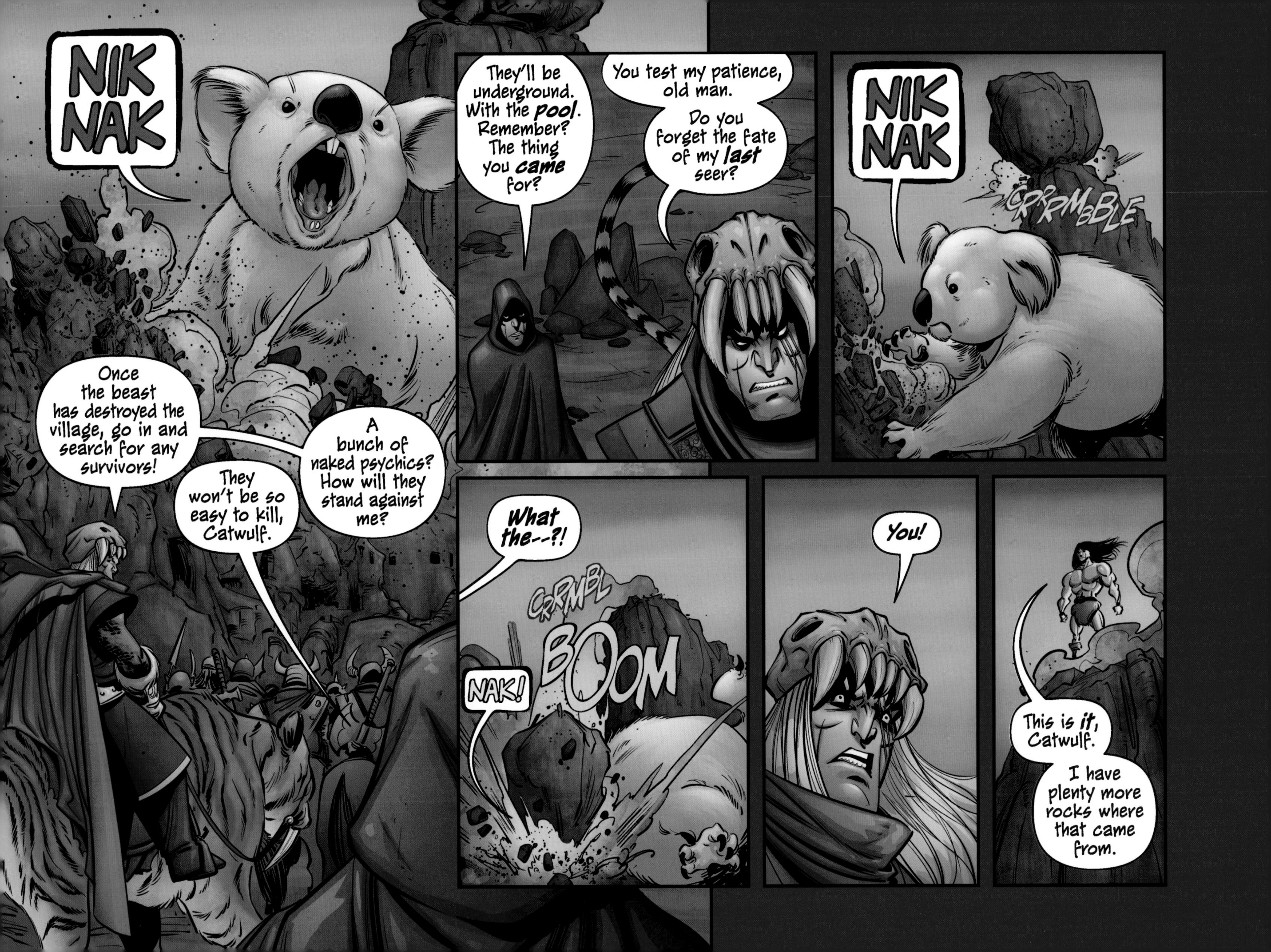

NIK NAK
Once the beast has destroyed the village, go in and search for any survivors!
A bunch of naked psychics? How will they stand against me?
They won't be so easy to kill, Catwulf.
They'll be underground. With the *pool*. Remember? The thing you *came* for?
You test my patience, old man.
Do you forget the fate of my *last* seer?
NIK NAK
CRRRMBBLE
What the--?!
CRRMBL
BOOM
NAK!
You!
This is *it*, Catwulf.
I have plenty more rocks where that came from.

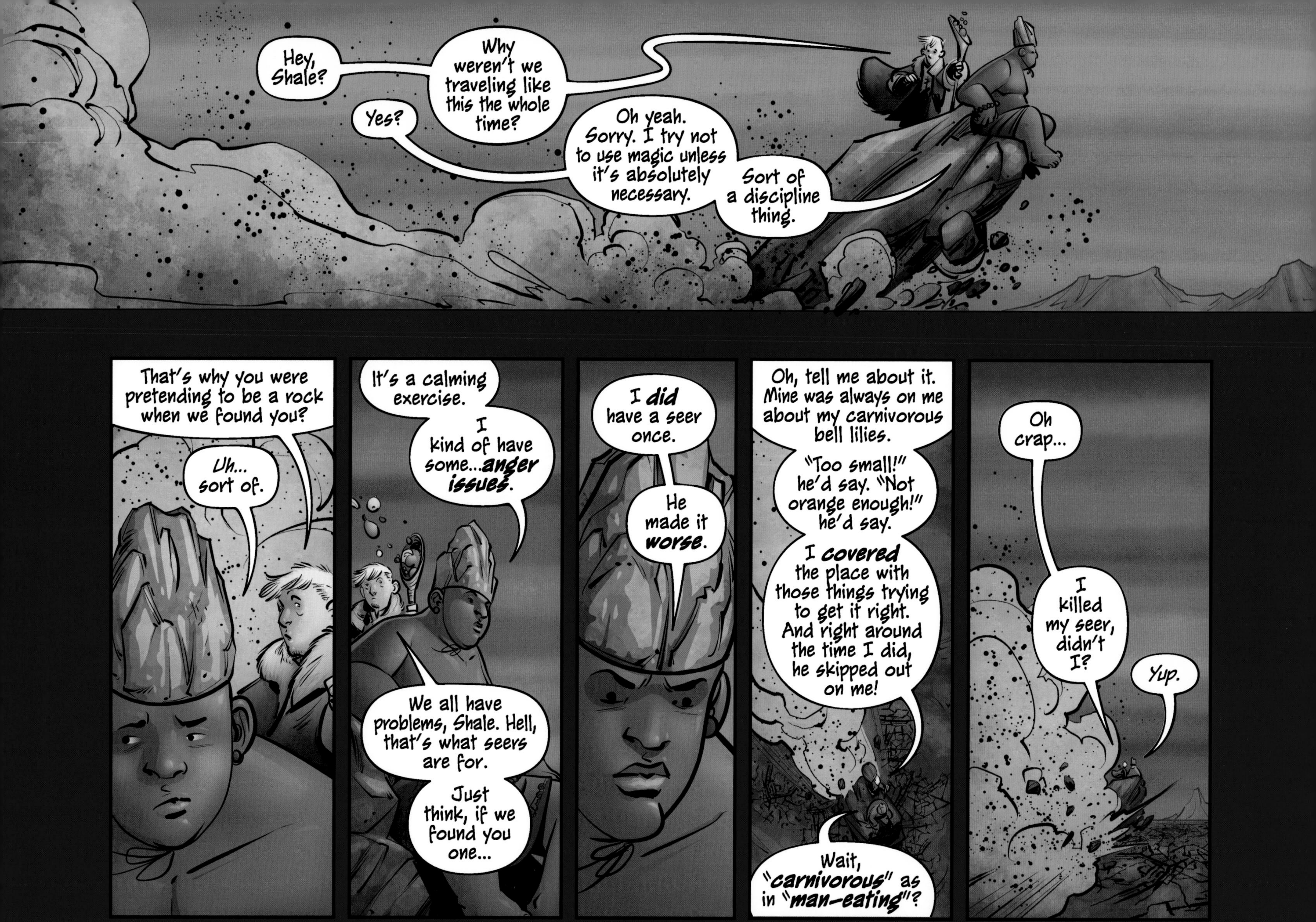
Hey, Shale?
Why weren't we traveling like this the whole time?
Yes?
Oh yeah. Sorry. I try not to use magic unless it's absolutely necessary.
Sort of a discipline thing.
That's why you were pretending to be a rock when we found you?
Uh... sort of.
It's a calming exercise.
I kind of have some...anger issues.
We all have problems, Shale. Hell, that's what seers are for.
Just think, if we found you one...
I did have a seer once.
He made it worse.
Oh, tell me about it. Mine was always on me about my carnivorous bell lilies.
"Too small!" he'd say. "Not orange enough!" he'd say.
I covered the place with those things trying to get it right. And right around the time I did, he skipped out on me!
Wait, "carnivorous" as in "man-eating"?
Oh crap...
I killed my seer, didn't I?
Yup.

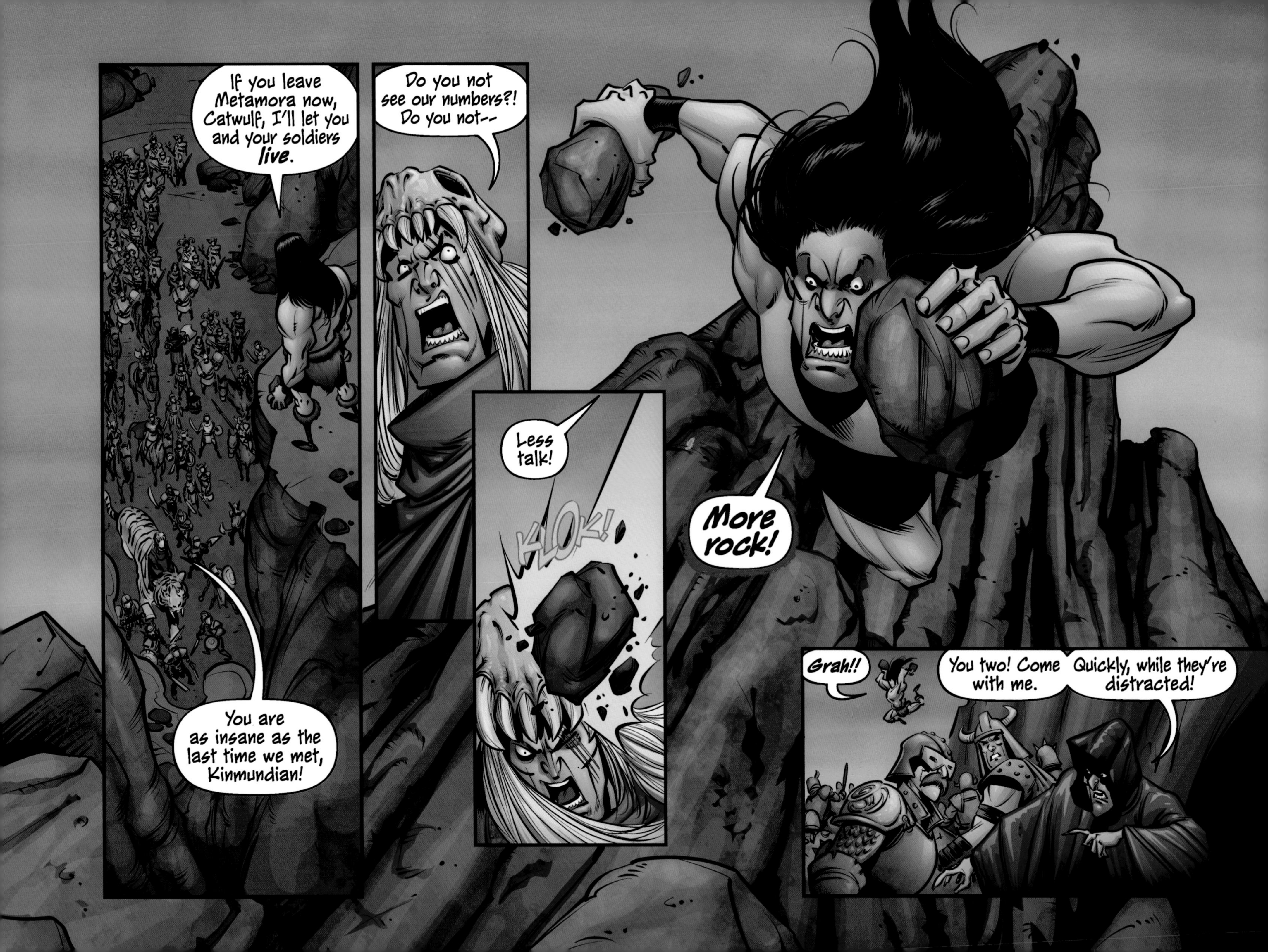
If you leave Metamora now, Catwulf, I'll let you and your soldiers *live*.
You are as insane as the last time we met, Kinmundian!
Do you not see our numbers?! Do you not--
Less talk!
KLOK!
More rock!
Grah!!
You two! Come with me.
Quickly, while they're distracted!

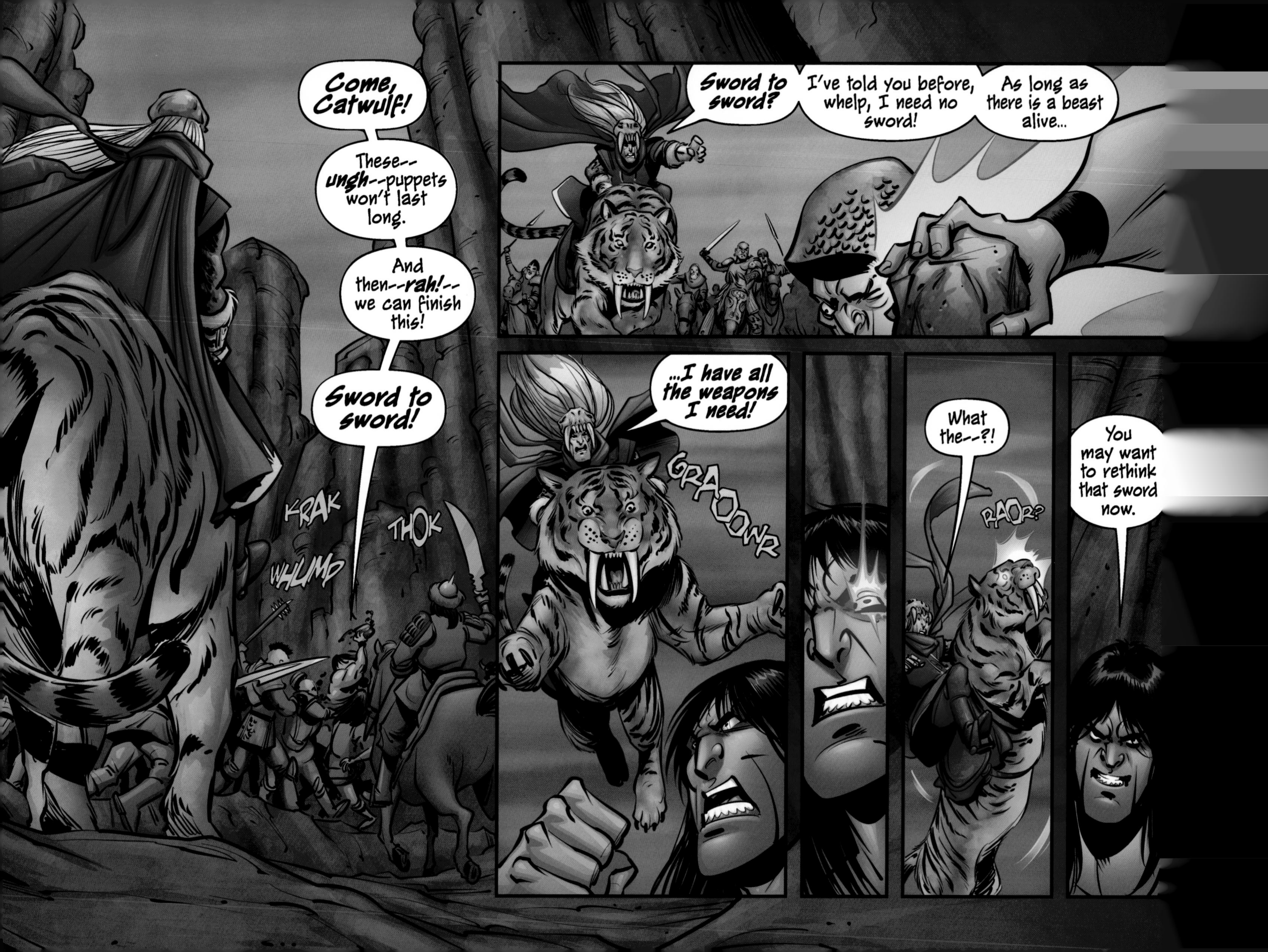
Come, Catwulf!
These--ungh--puppets won't last long.
And then--rah!--we can finish this!
Sword to sword!
KRAK
THOK
WHUMP
Sword to sword?
I've told you before, whelp, I need no sword!
As long as there is a beast alive...
...I have all the weapons I need!
GRAOOWR
What the--?!
RAOR?
You may want to rethink that sword now.

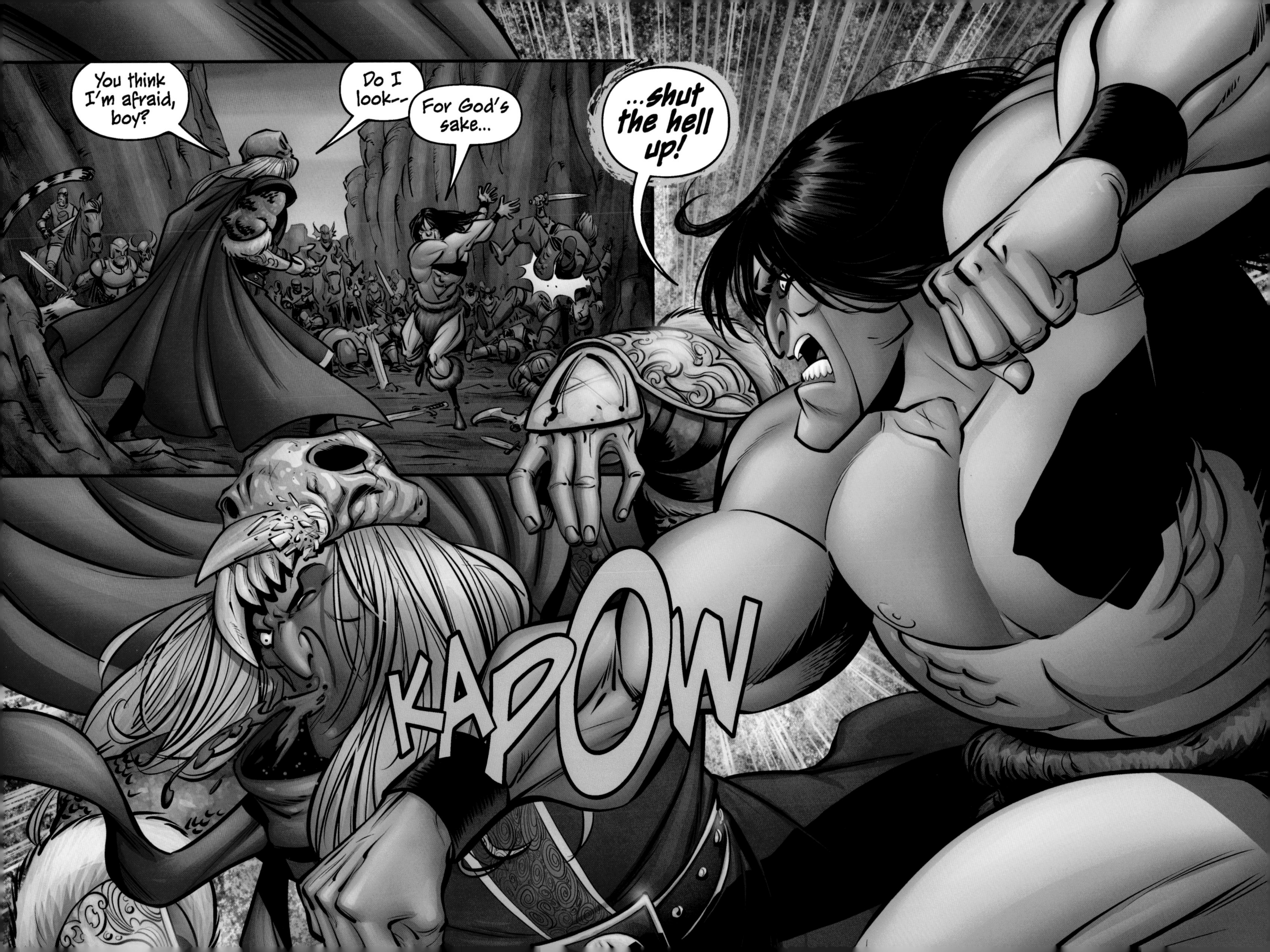
You think I'm afraid, boy?
Do I look--
For God's sake...
...shut the hell up!
KAPOW

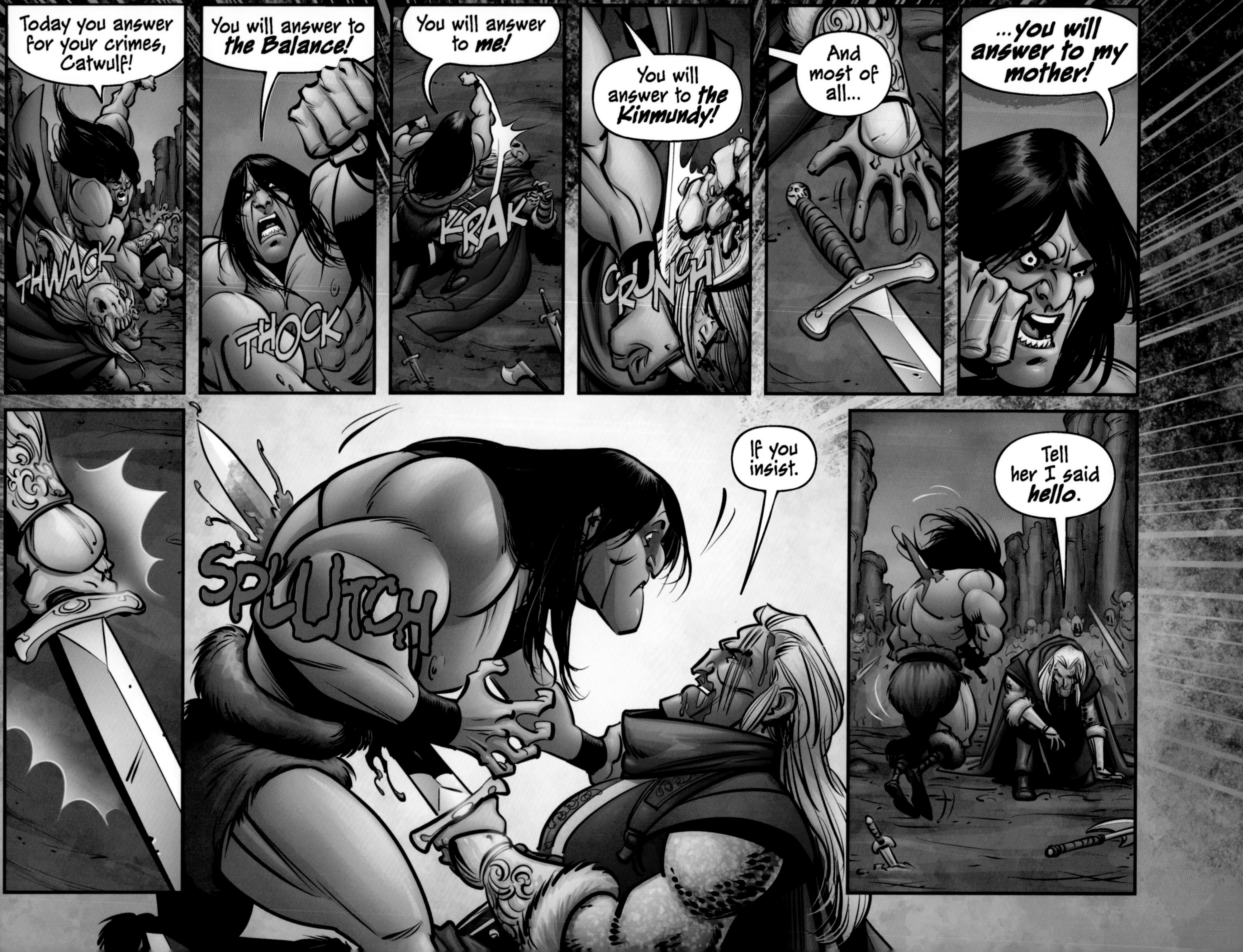
Today you answer for your crimes, Catwulf!
THWACK
You will answer to the Balance!
THOCK
You will answer to me!
KRAK
You will answer to the Kinmundy!
CRUNCH
And most of all...
...you will answer to my mother!
SPLUTCH
If you insist.
Tell her I said hello.

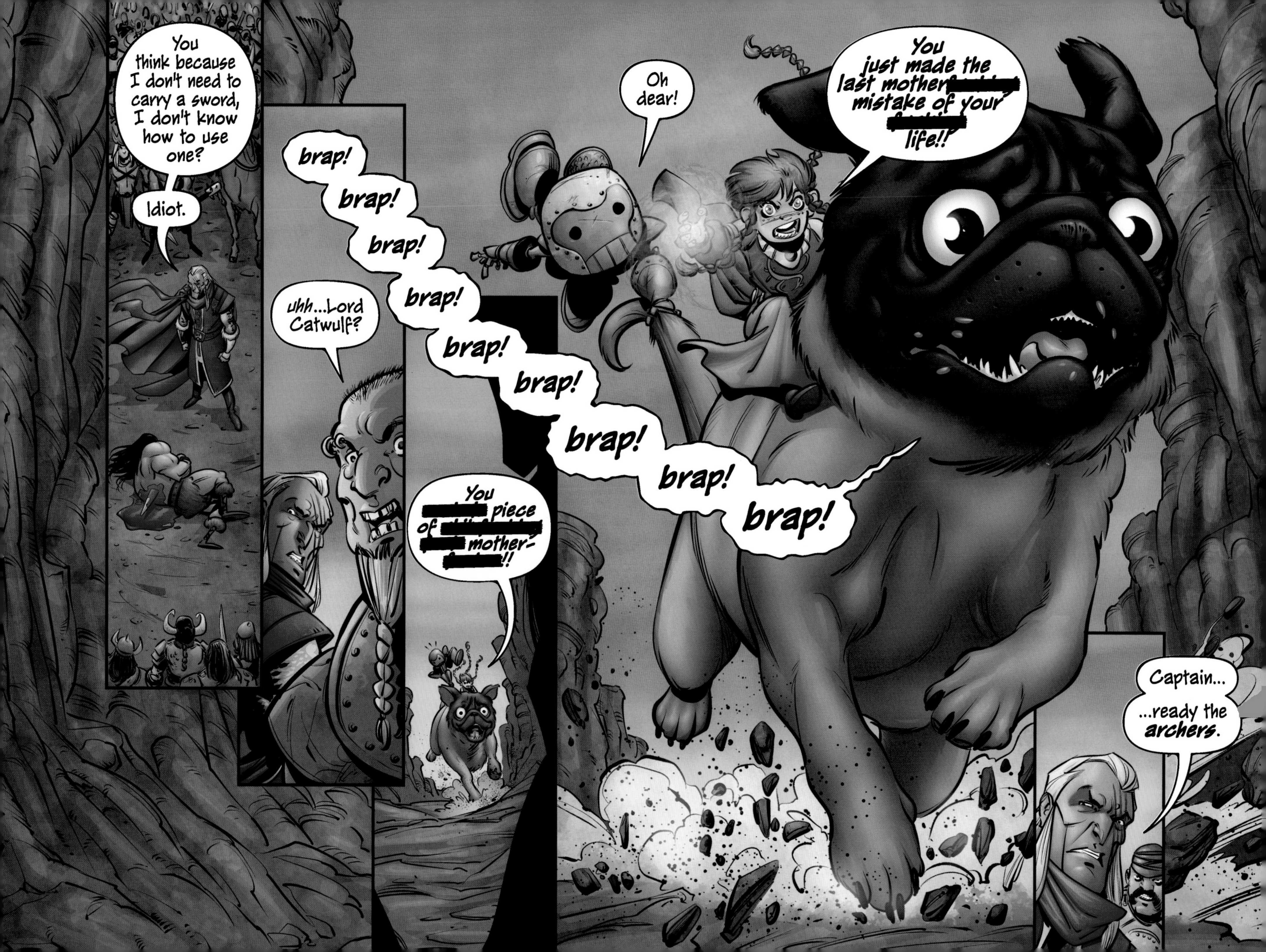

You think because I don't need to carry a sword, I don't know how to use one?
Idiot.
brap!
brap!
brap!
brap!
brap!
brap!
brap!
brap!
brap!
uhh...Lord Catwulf?
You [redacted] piece of [redacted] mother-[redacted]!!
Oh dear!
You just made the last mother[redacted] mistake of your [redacted] life!!
Captain...
...ready the archers.

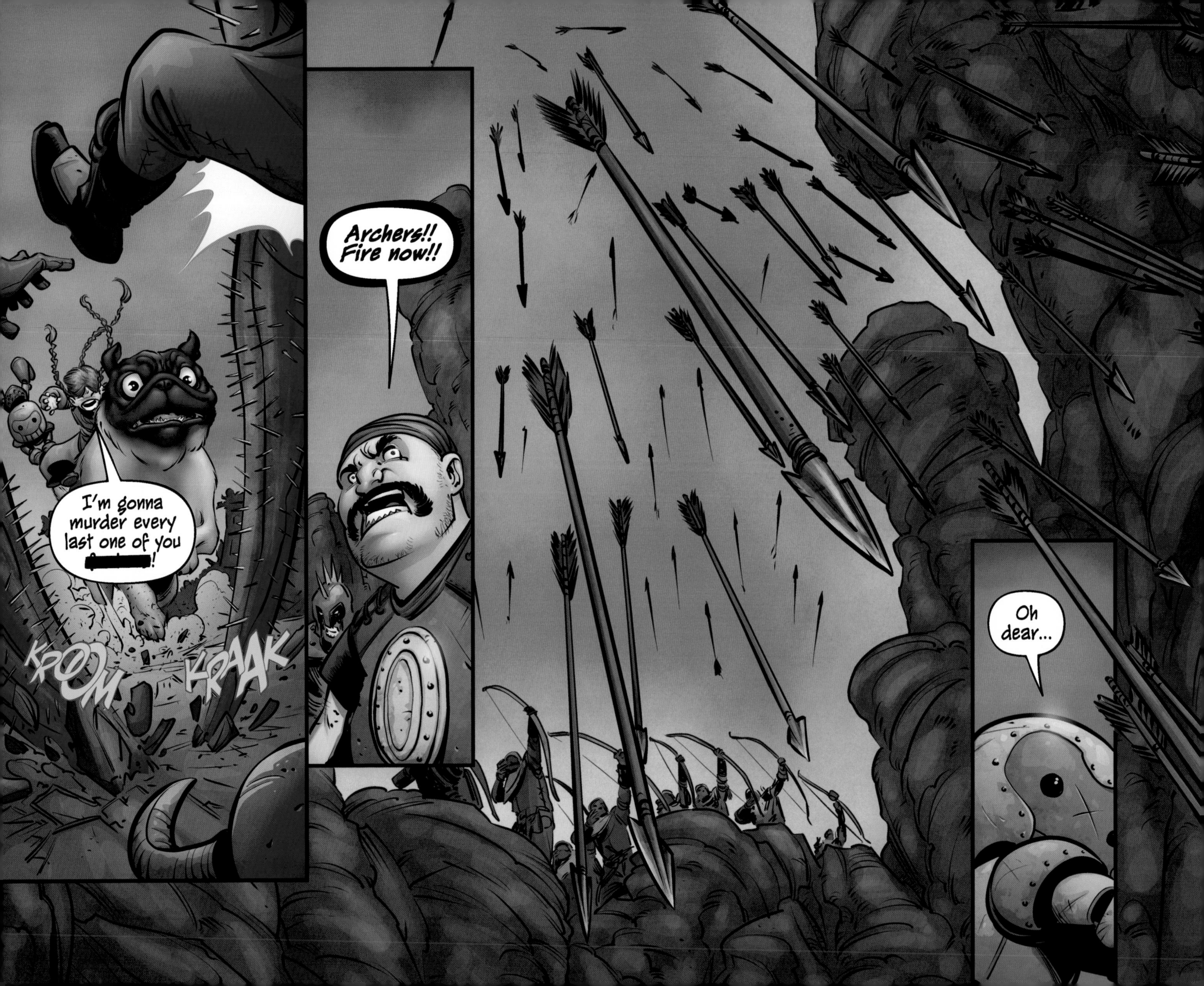
I'm gonna murder every last one of you [redacted]!
KROOM
KRAAK
Archers!! Fire now!!
Oh dear...

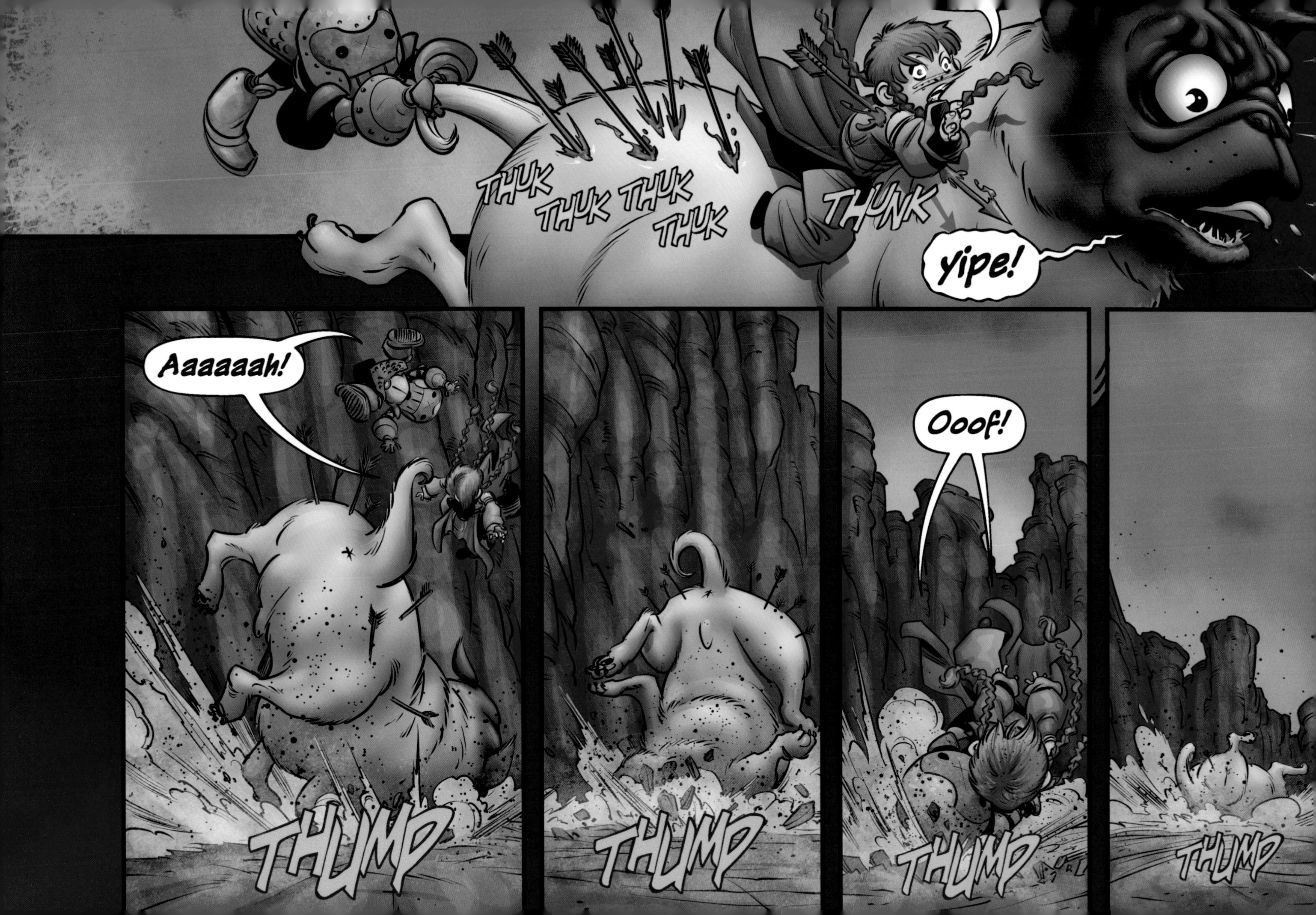

THUK
THUK THUK
THUK
THUNK
yipe!
Aaaaaah!
THUMP
THUMP
Ooof!
THUMP
THUMP

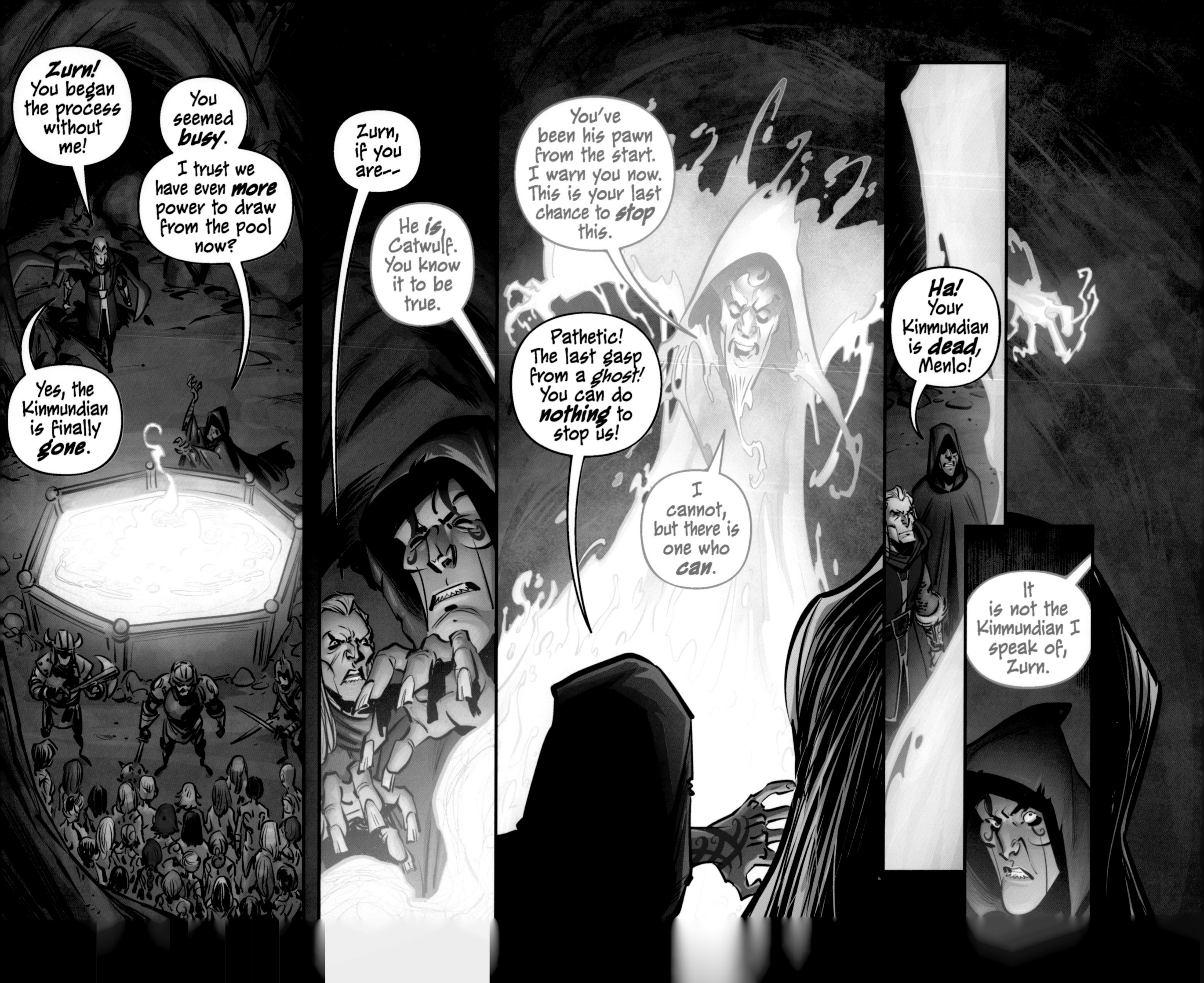

Zurn! You began the process without me!
You seemed busy.
I trust we have even more power to draw from the pool now?
Yes, the Kinmundian is finally gone.
Zurn, if you are--
He is Catwulf. You know it to be true.
You've been his pawn from the start. I warn you now. This is your last chance to stop this.
Pathetic! The last gasp from a ghost! You can do nothing to stop us!
I cannot, but there is one who can.
Ha! Your Kinmundian is dead, Menlo!
It is not the Kinmundian I speak of, Zurn.

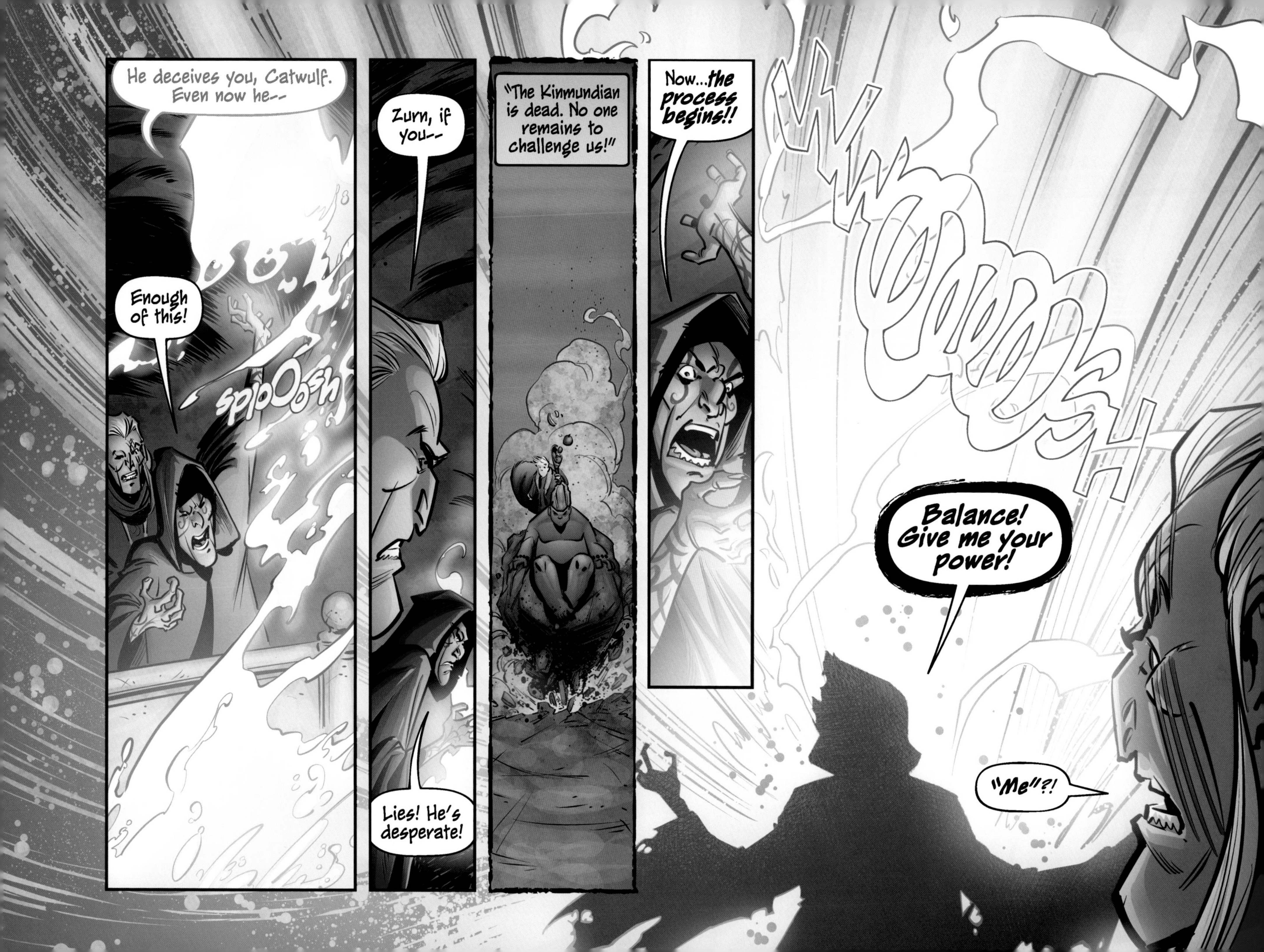
He deceives you, Catwulf. Even now he--
Enough of this!
SPLOOOSH
Zurn, if you--
Lies! He's desperate!
"The Kinmundian is dead. No one remains to challenge us!"
Now...the process begins!!
WHOOOOOSH
Balance! Give me your power!
"Me"?!

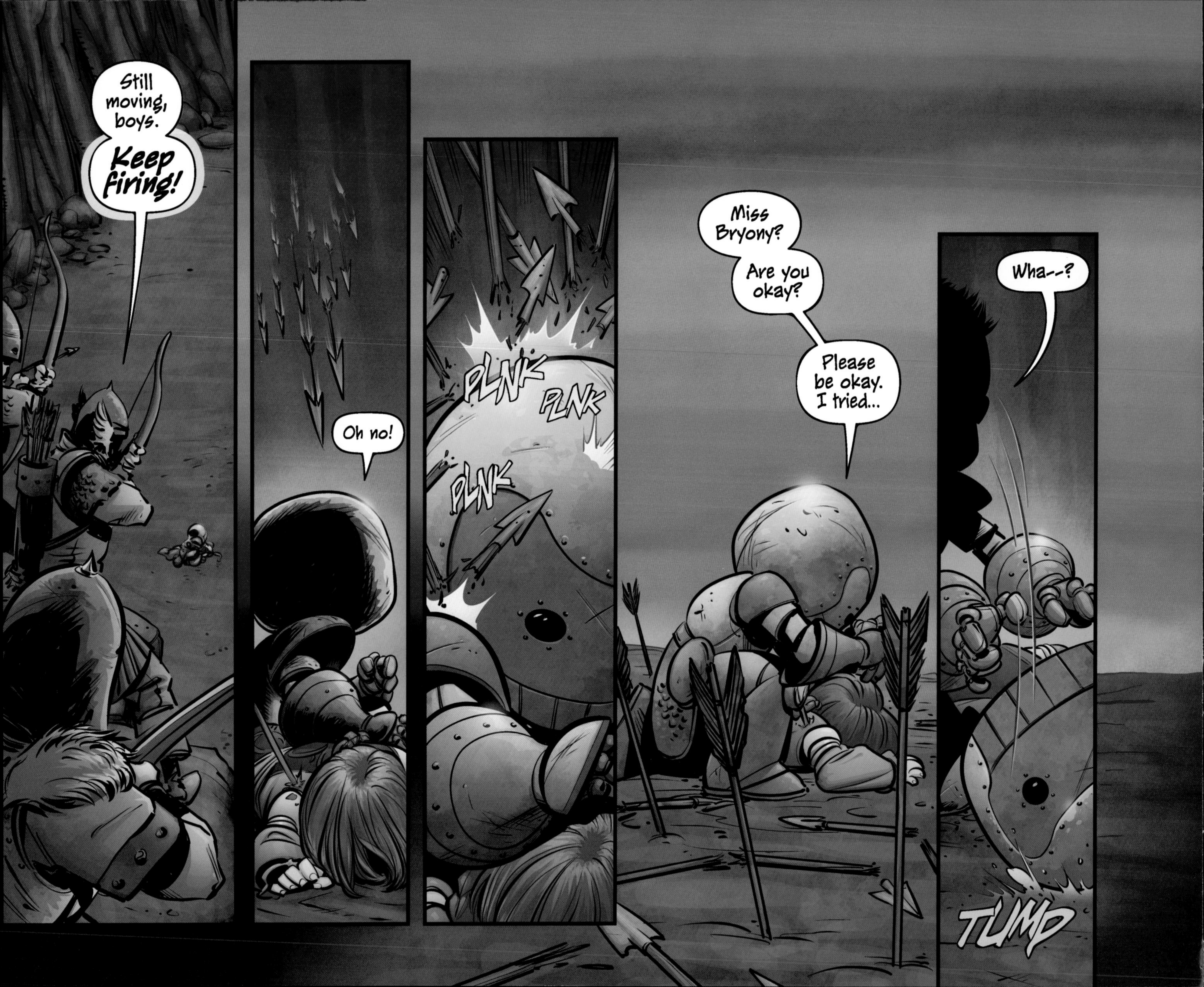
Still moving, boys.
Keep firing!
Oh no!
PLNK
PLNK
PLNK
Miss Bryony?
Are you okay?
Please be okay. I tried...
Wha--?
TUMP

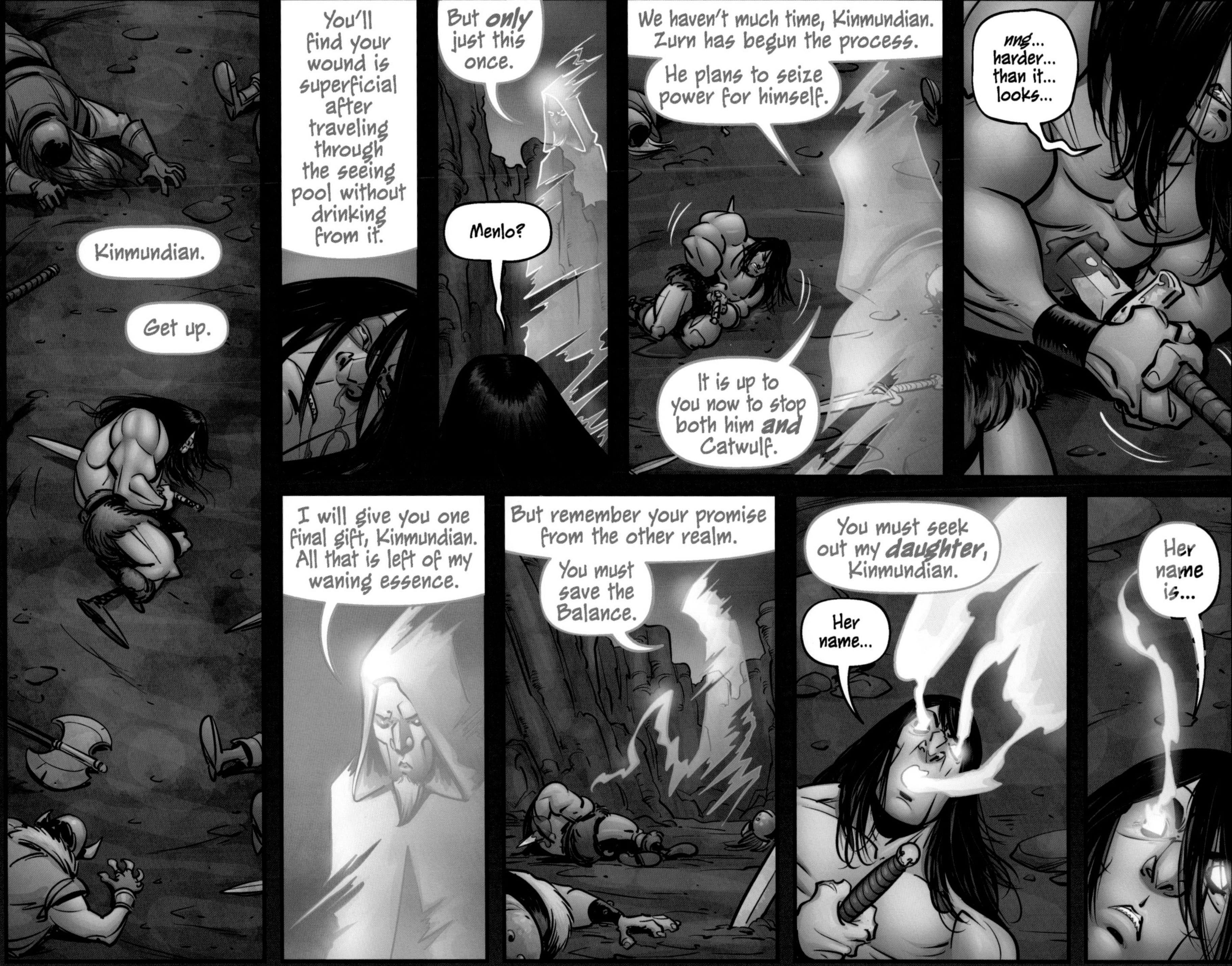

Kinmundian.
Get up.
You'll find your wound is superficial after traveling through the seeing pool without drinking from it.
But only just this once.
Menlo?
We haven't much time, Kinmundian. Zurn has begun the process.
He plans to seize power for himself.
It is up to you now to stop both him and Catwulf.
nng... harder... than it... looks...
I will give you one final gift, Kinmundian. All that is left of my waning essence.
But remember your promise from the other realm.
You must save the Balance.
You must seek out my daughter, Kinmundian.
Her name...
Her name is...

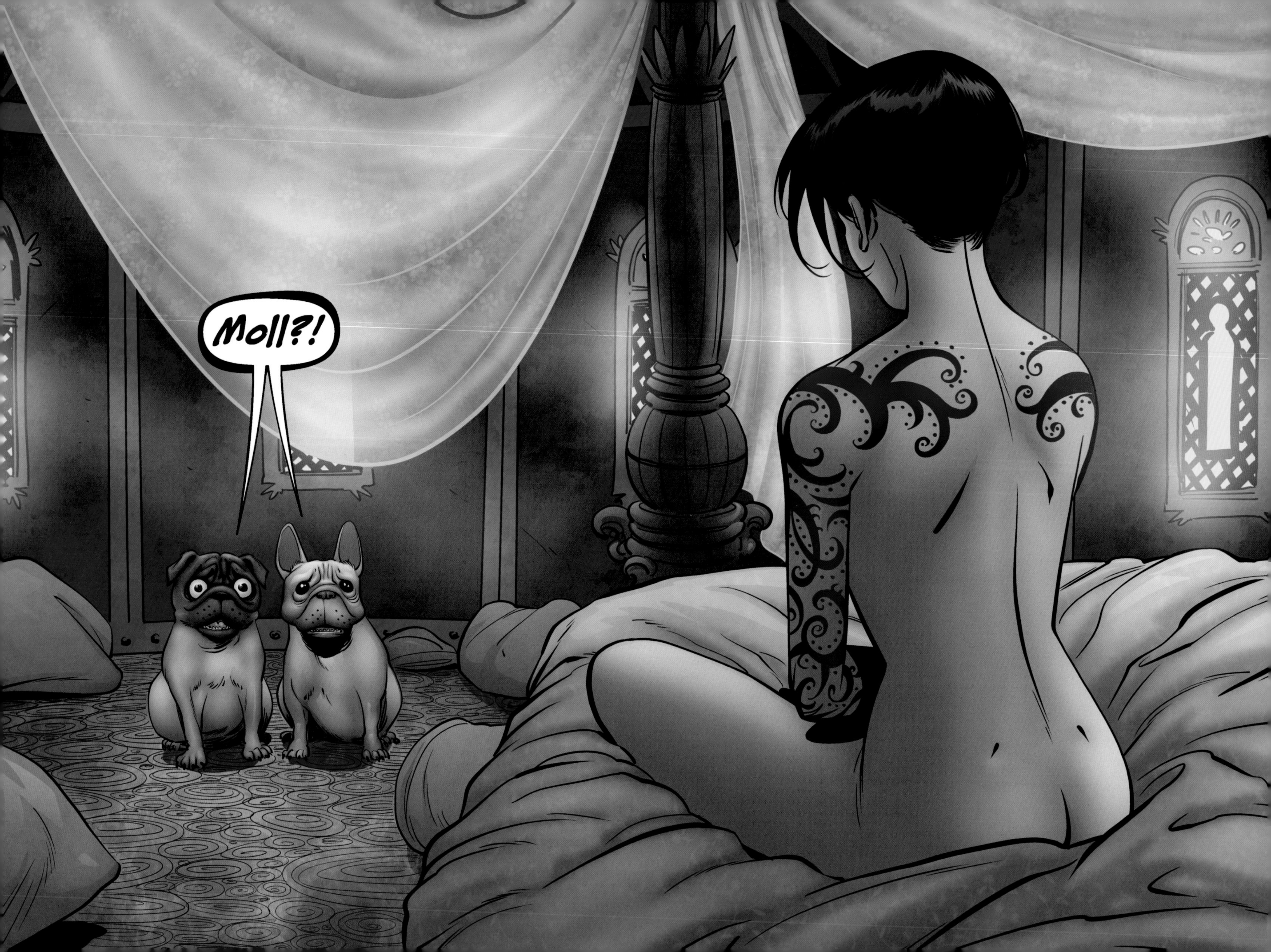
Moll?!

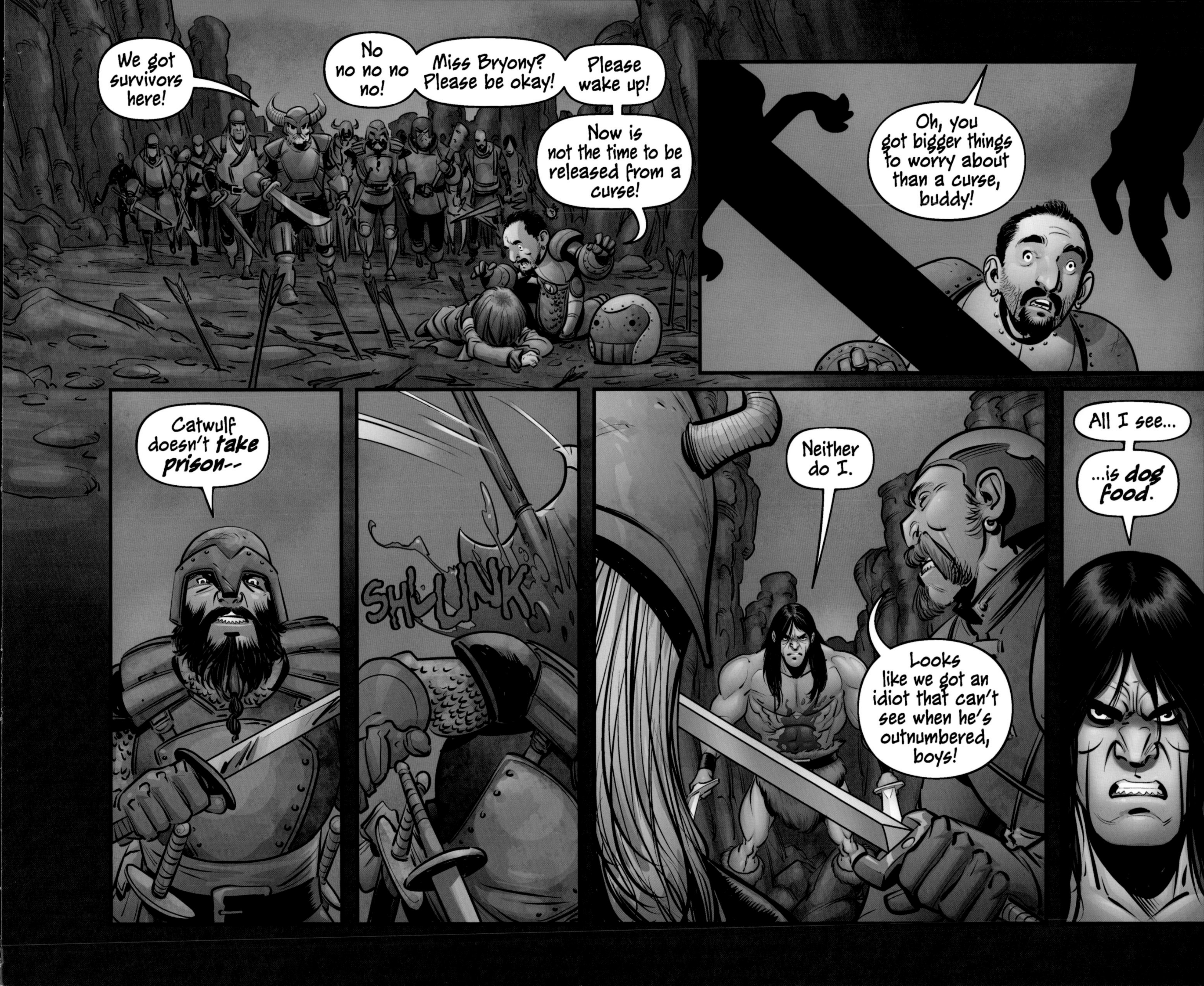

We got survivors here!
No no no no no!
Miss Bryony? Please be okay!
Please wake up!
Now is not the time to be released from a curse!
Oh, you got bigger things to worry about than a curse, buddy!
Catwulf doesn't **take prison--**
SHLUNK
Neither do I.
Looks like we got an idiot that can't see when he's outnumbered, boys!
All I see...
...is **dog food**.

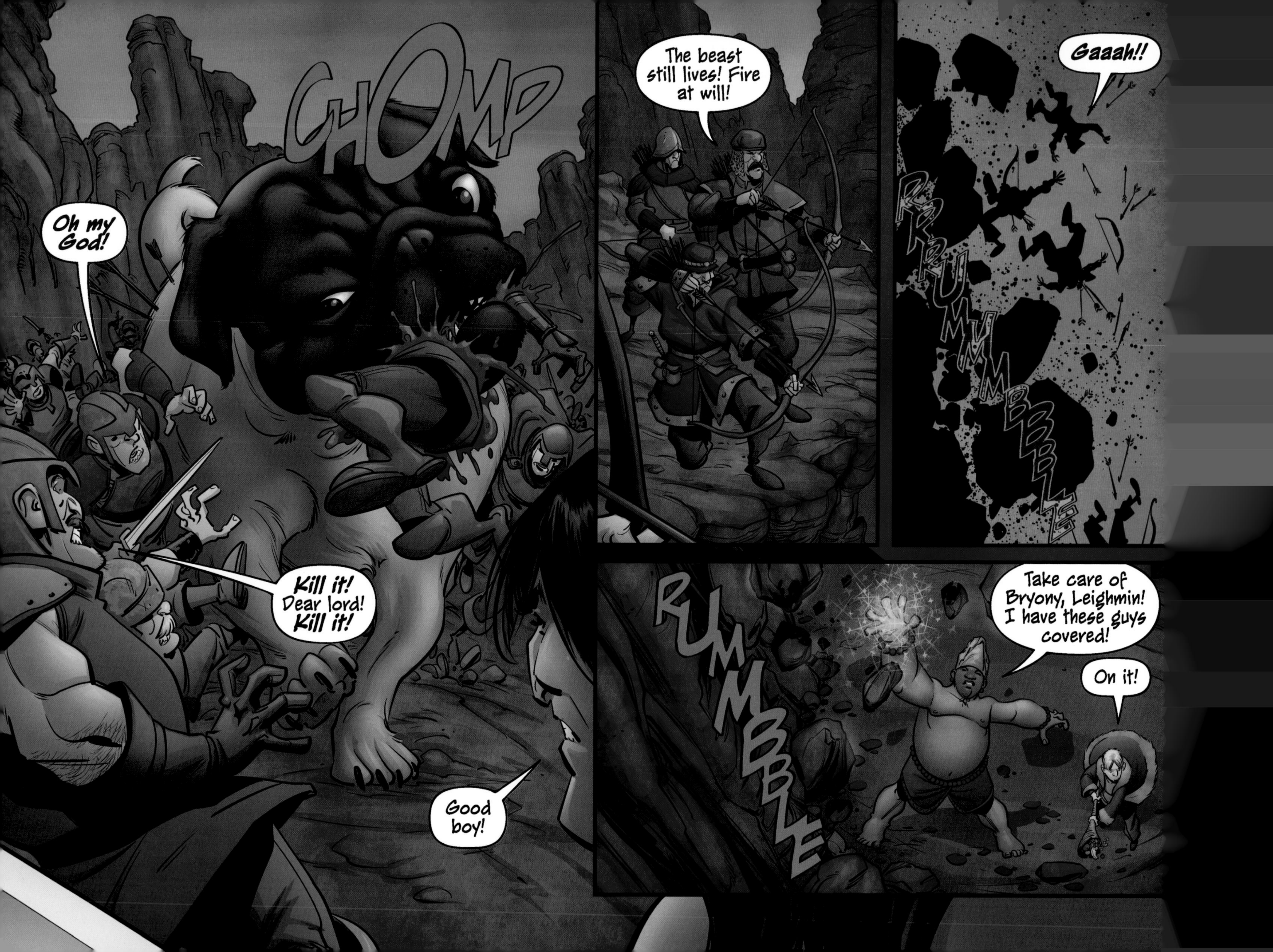
CHOMP
Oh my God!
Kill it! Dear lord! Kill it!
Good boy!
The beast still lives! Fire at will!
Gaaah!!
RRRUMMMBBBLLE
RUMMBBLE
Take care of Bryony, Leighmin! I have these guys covered!
On it!

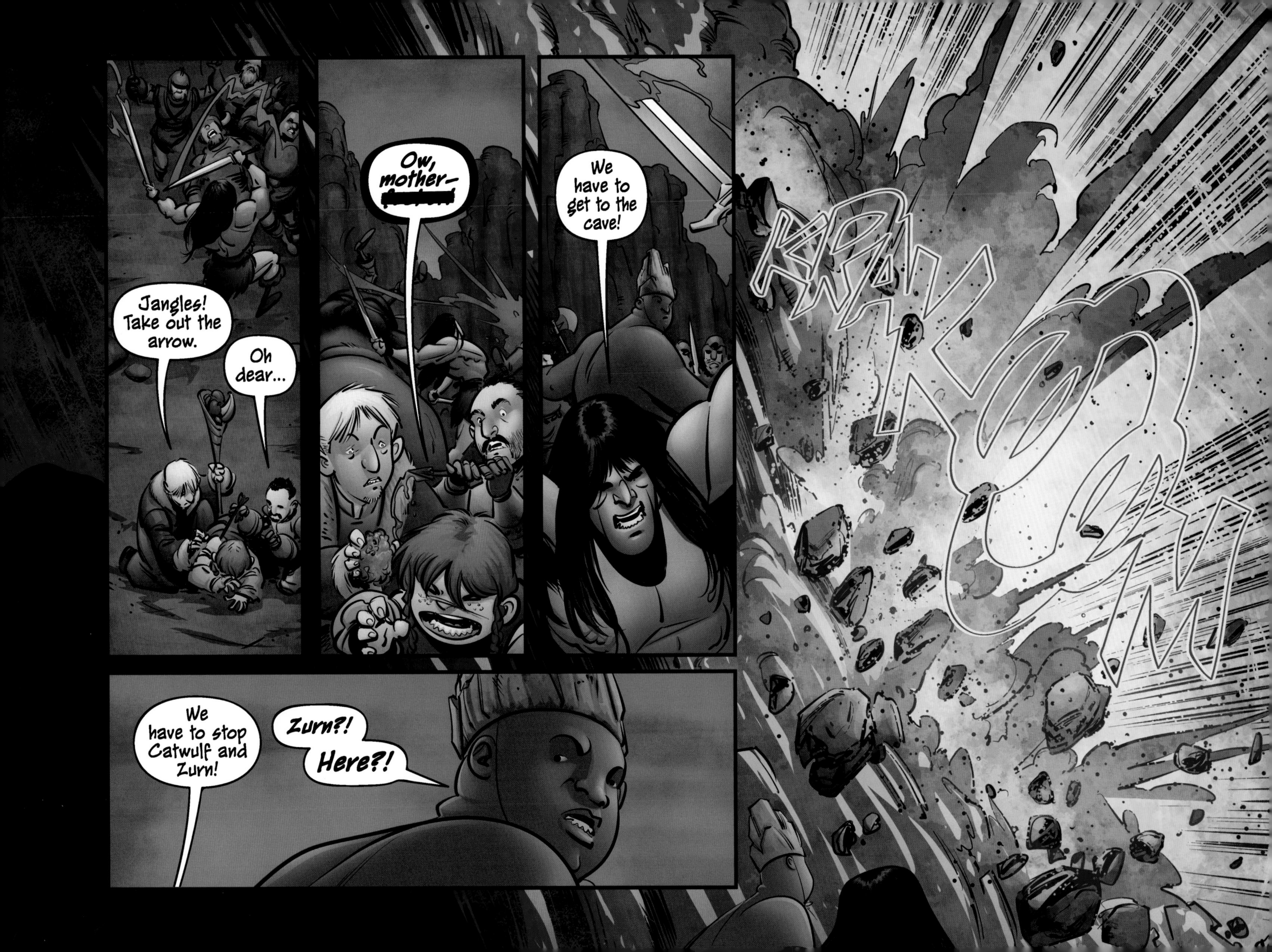
Jangles! Take out the arrow.
Oh dear...
Ow, mother-[redacted]
We have to get to the cave!
We have to stop Catwulf and Zurn!
Zurn?! Here?!

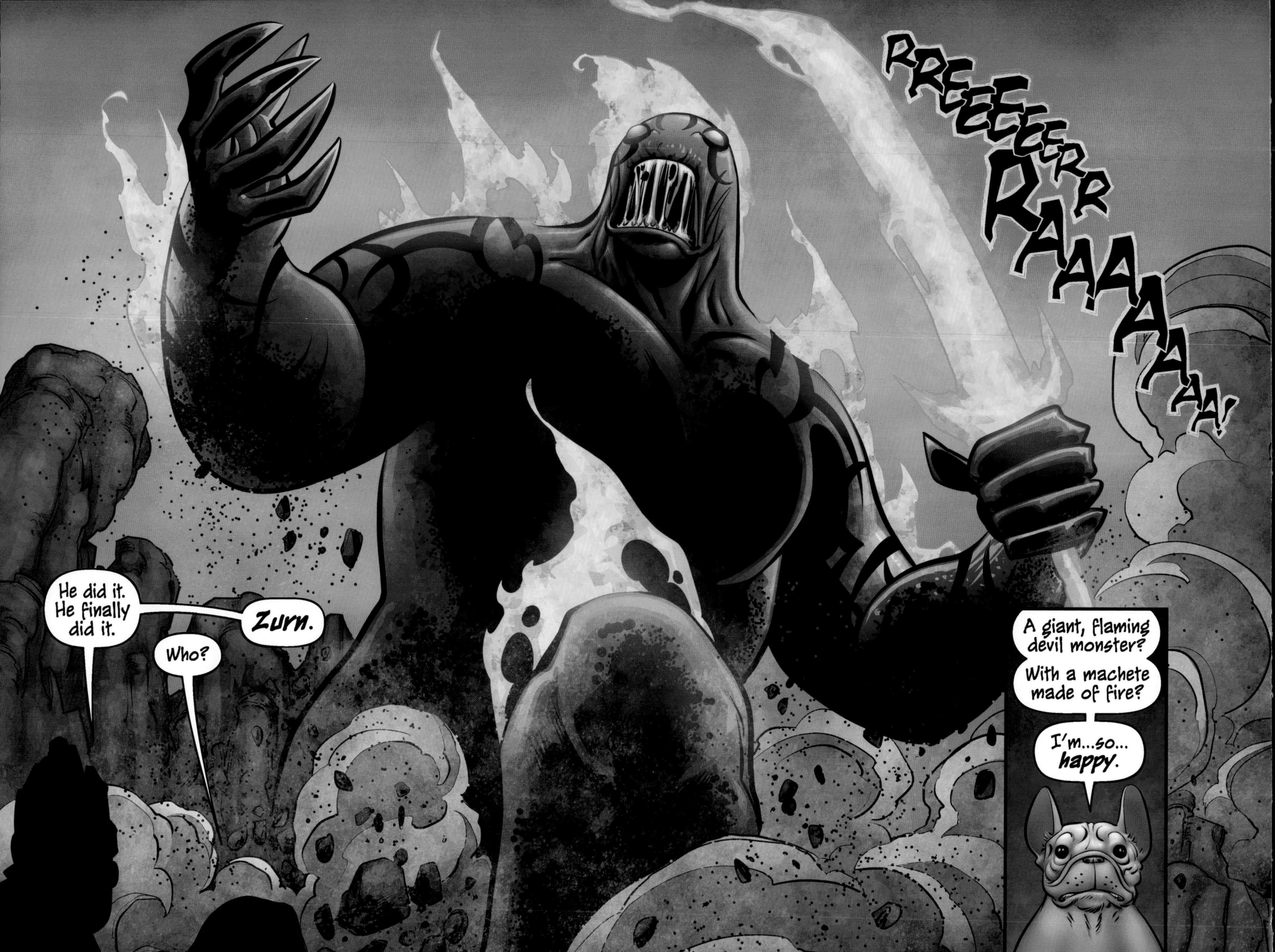
RREEEEEERRRAAAAAAAA!
He did it. He finally did it.
Zurn.
Who?
A giant, flaming devil monster?
With a machete made of fire?
I'm...so... happy.

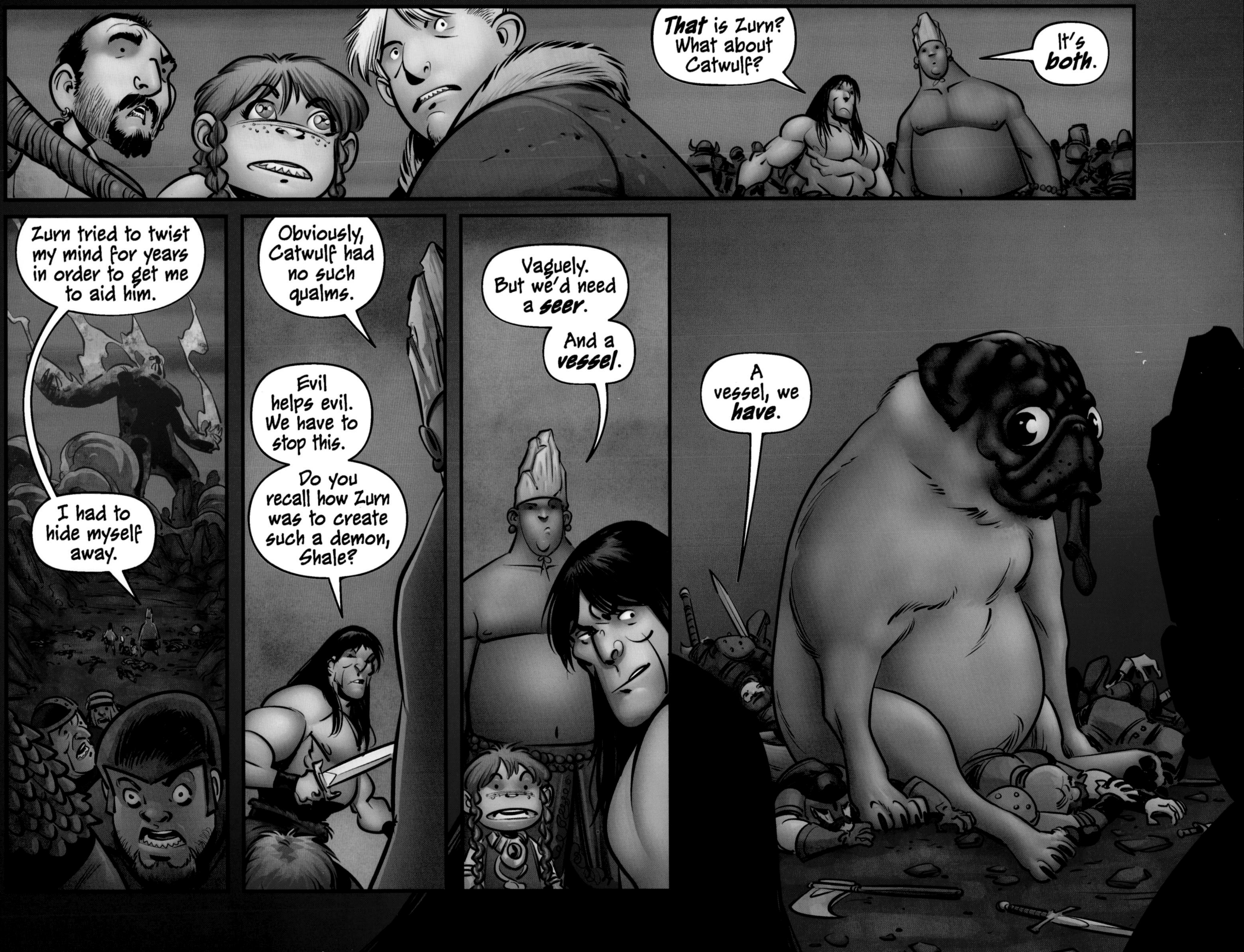

That is Zurn? What about Catwulf?
It's both.
Zurn tried to twist my mind for years in order to get me to aid him.
I had to hide myself away.
Obviously, Catwulf had no such qualms.
Evil helps evil. We have to stop this.
Do you recall how Zurn was to create such a demon, Shale?
Vaguely. But we'd need a seer.
And a vessel.
A vessel, we have.

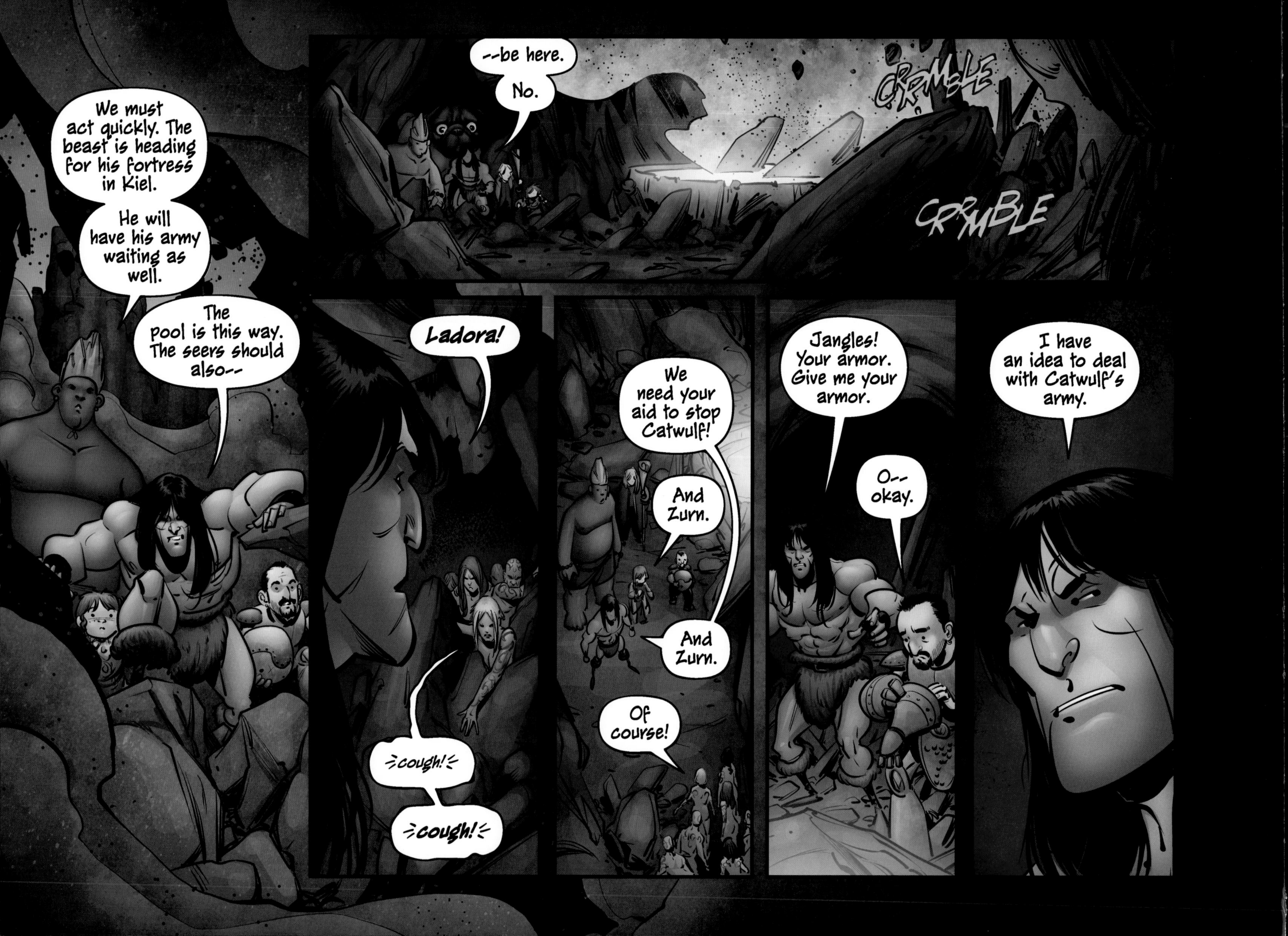
We must act quickly. The beast is heading for his fortress in Kiel.
He will have his army waiting as well.
The pool is this way. The seers should also--
--be here.
No.
CRRMBLE
CRRMBLE
Ladora!
cough!
cough!
We need your aid to stop Catwulf!
And Zurn.
And Zurn.
Of course!
Jangles! Your armor. Give me your armor.
O-- okay.
I have an idea to deal with Catwulf's army.

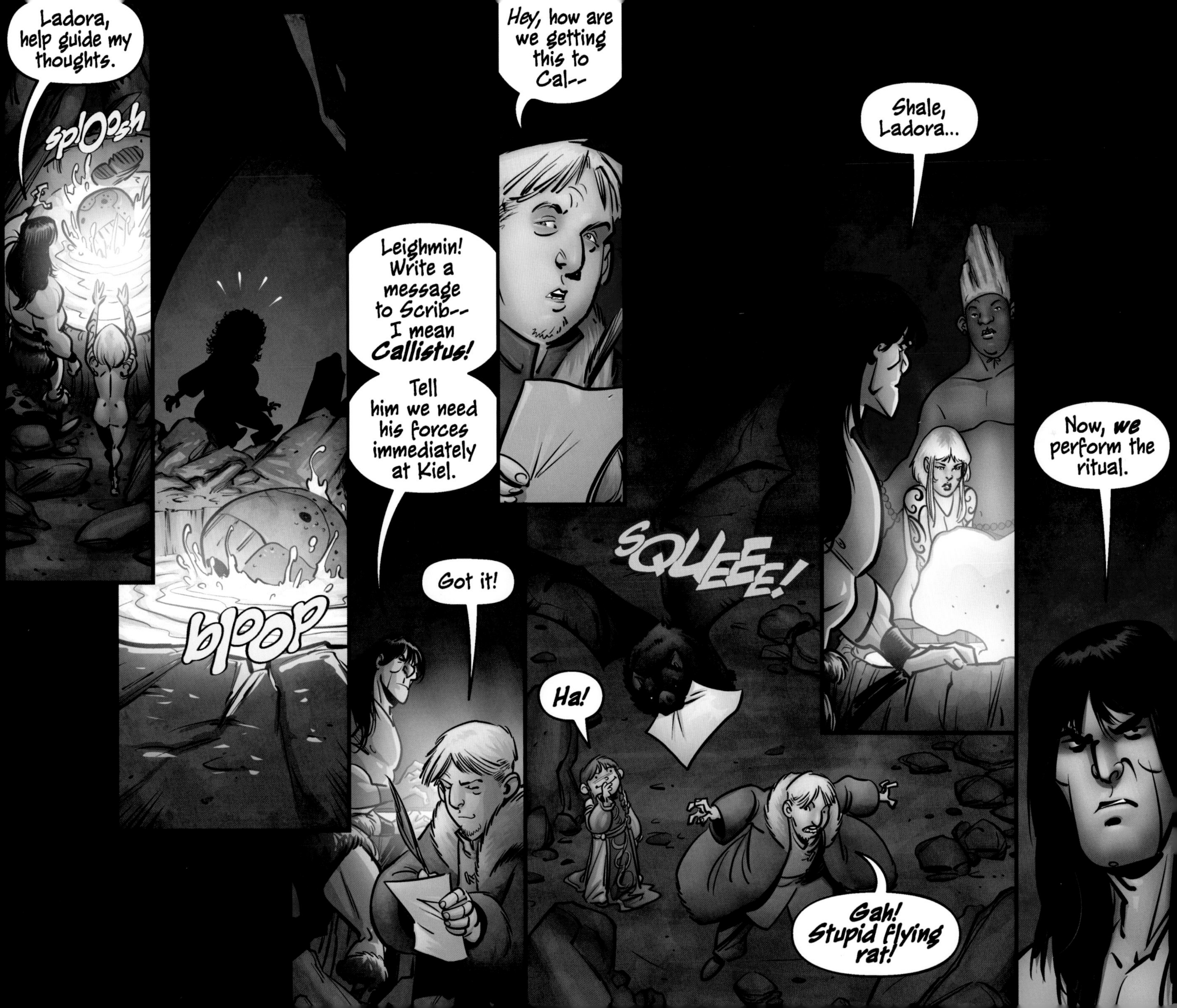
Ladora, help guide my thoughts.
splOOsh
bloop
Hey, how are we getting this to Cal--
Leighmin! Write a message to Scrib-- I mean Callistus!
Tell him we need his forces immediately at Kiel.
Got it!
SQUEEEE!
Ha!
Gah! Stupid flying rat!
Shale, Ladora...
Now, we perform the ritual.

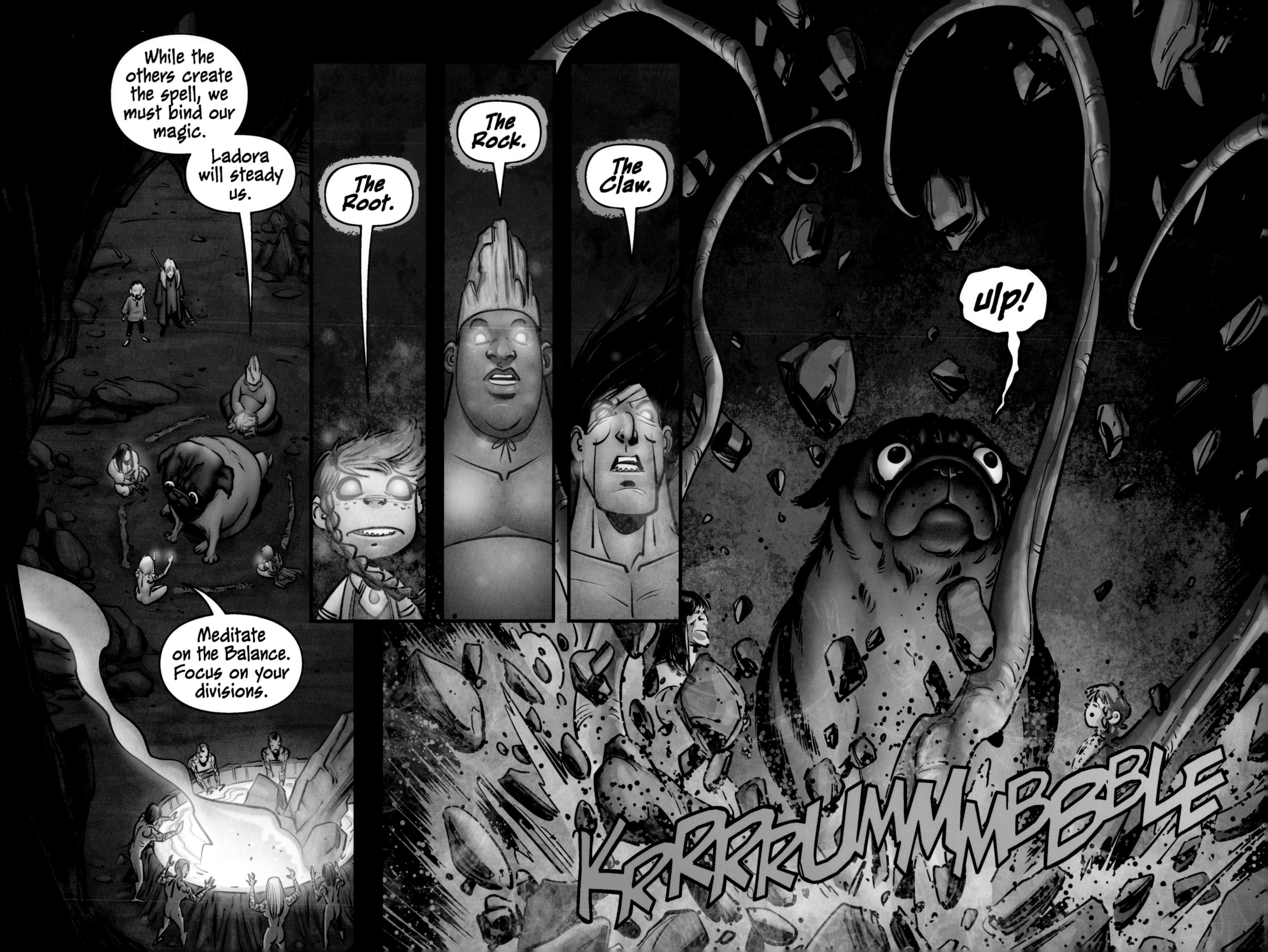
While the others create the spell, we must bind our magic.
Ladora will steady us.
Meditate on the Balance. Focus on your divisions.
The Root.
The Rock.
The Claw.
ulp!
KRRRRUMMMBBLE

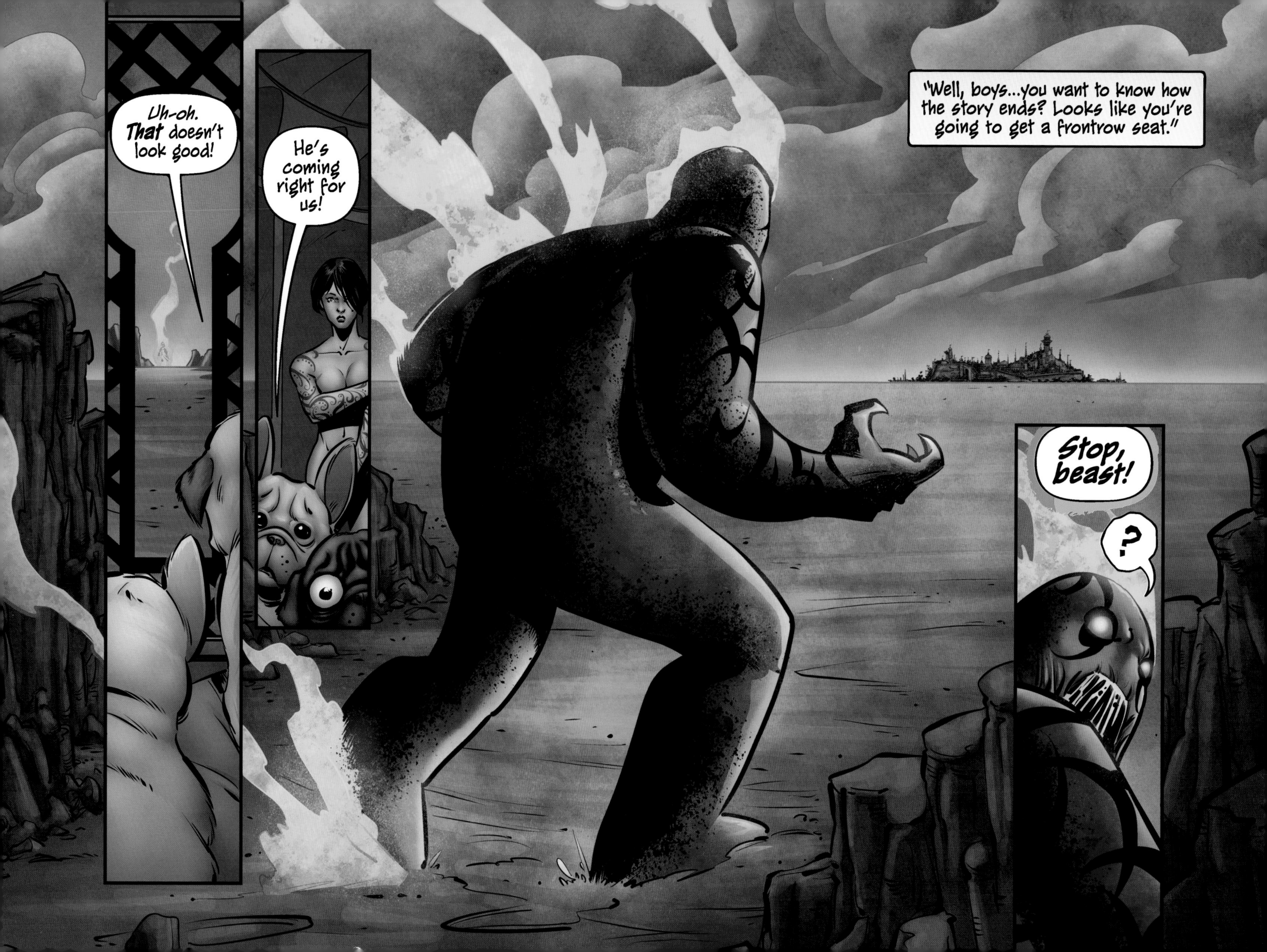
Uh-oh. That doesn't look good!
He's coming right for us!
"Well, boys...you want to know how the story ends? Looks like you're going to get a frontrow seat."
Stop, beast!
?

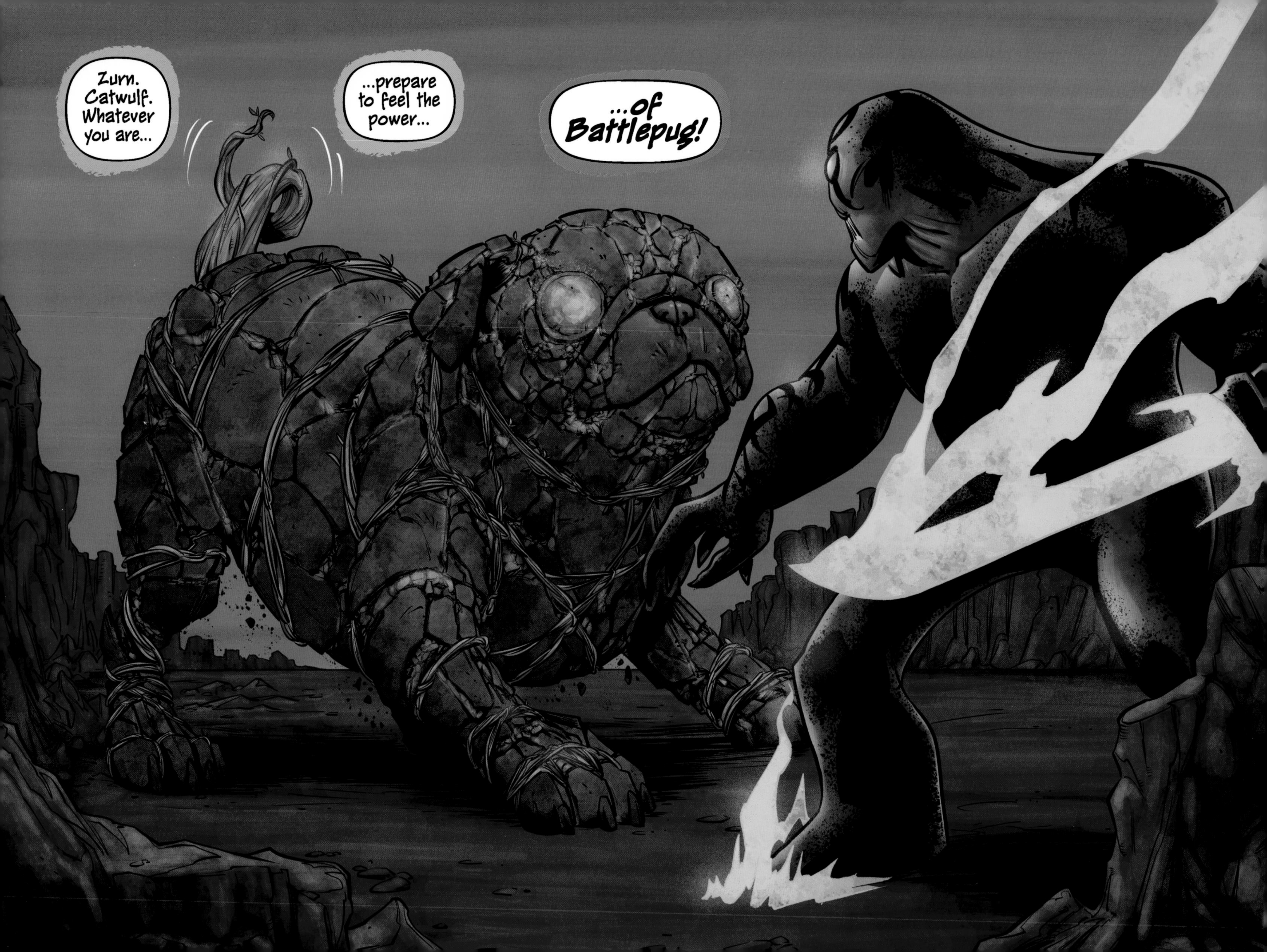
Zurn. Catwulf. Whatever you are...
...prepare to feel the power...
...of Battlepug!

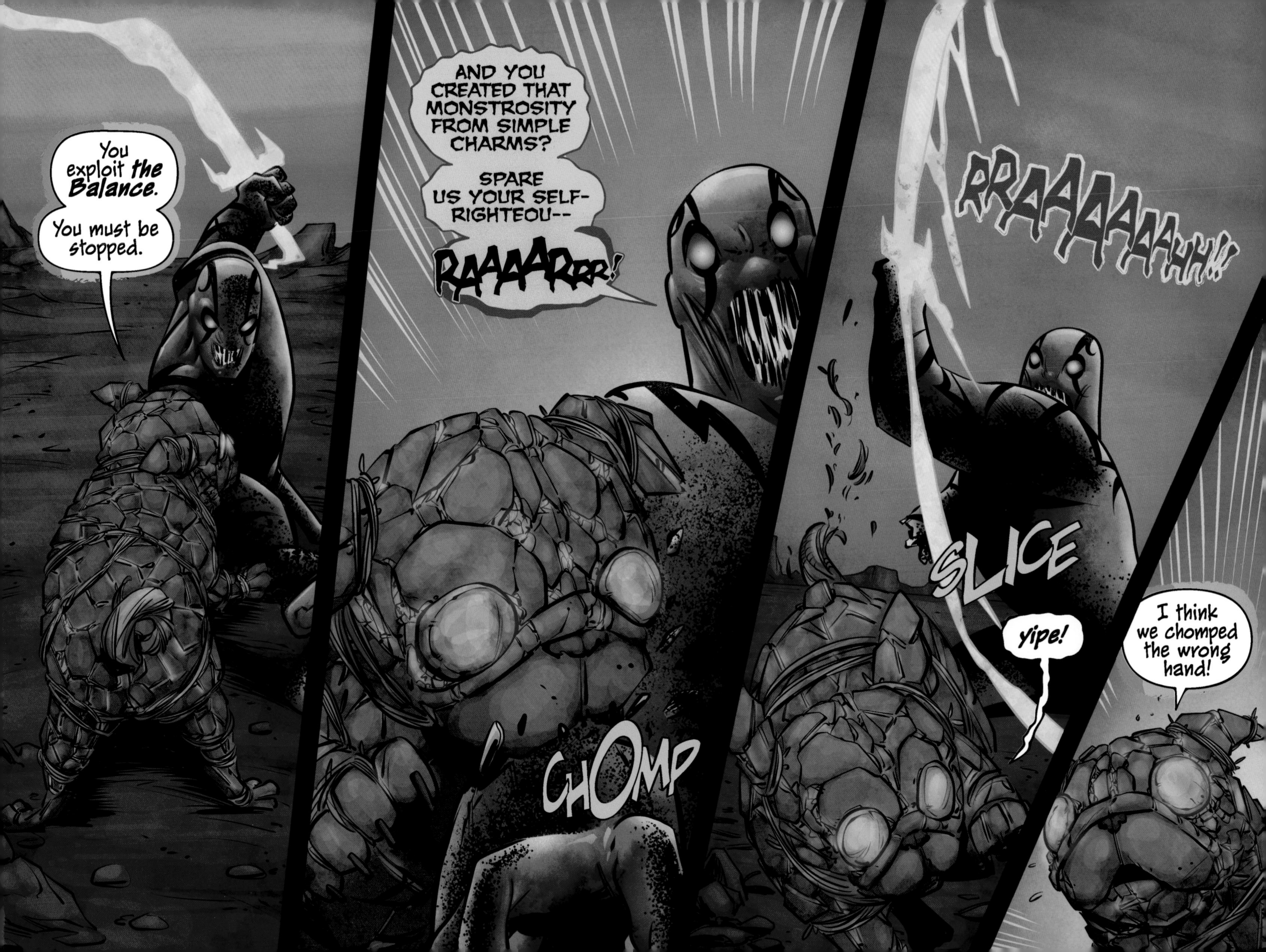
You exploit the Balance.
You must be stopped.
AND YOU CREATED THAT MONSTROSITY FROM SIMPLE CHARMS?
SPARE US YOUR SELF-RIGHTEOU--
RAAAARRR!
CHOMP
RRAAAAAAAHH!!
SLICE
yipe!
I think we chomped the wrong hand!

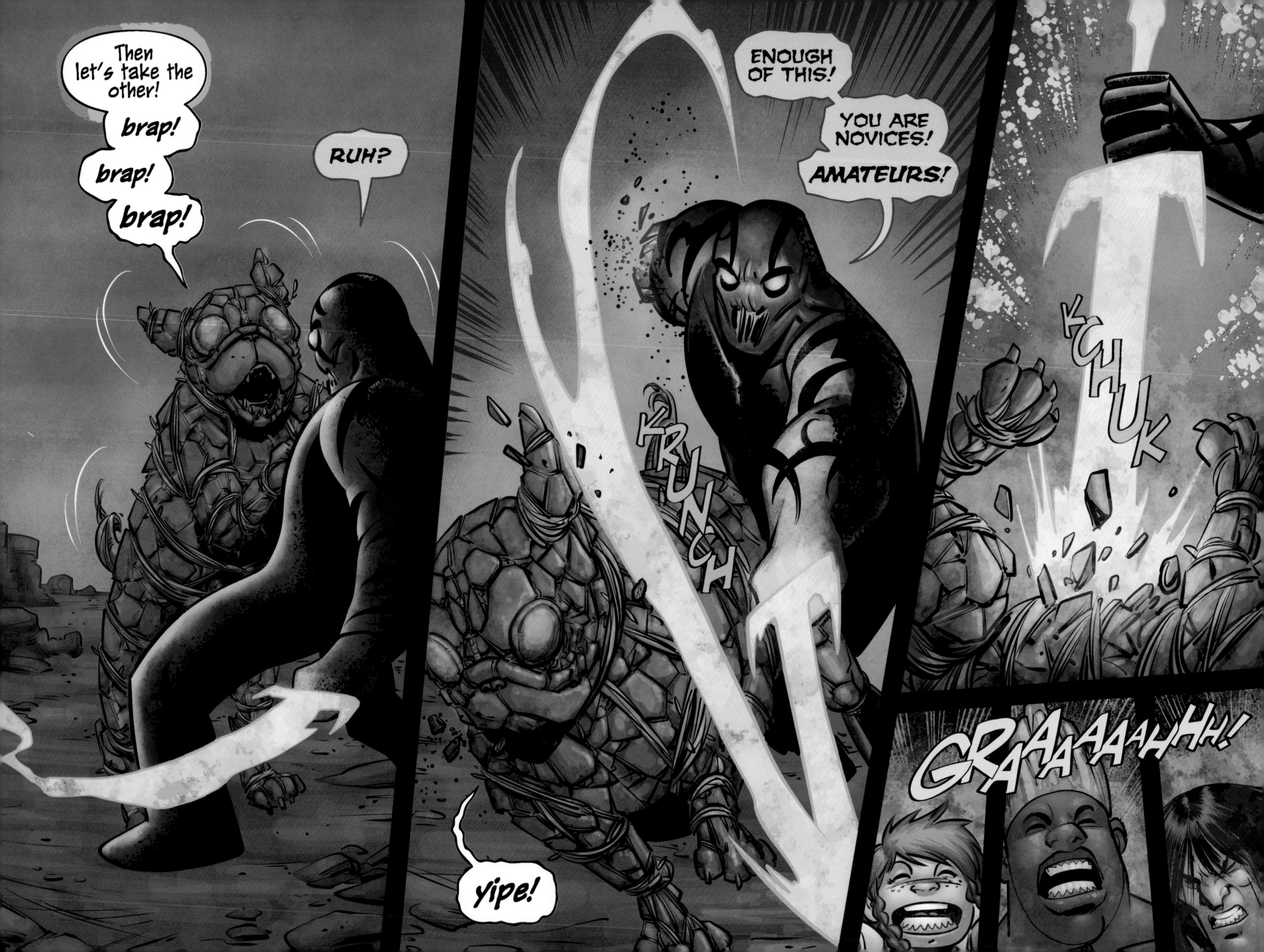

Then let's take the other!
brap!
brap!
brap!
RUH?
yipe!
ENOUGH OF THIS!
YOU ARE NOVICES!
AMATEURS!
KRUNCH
KCHUK
GRAAAAAAHHH!

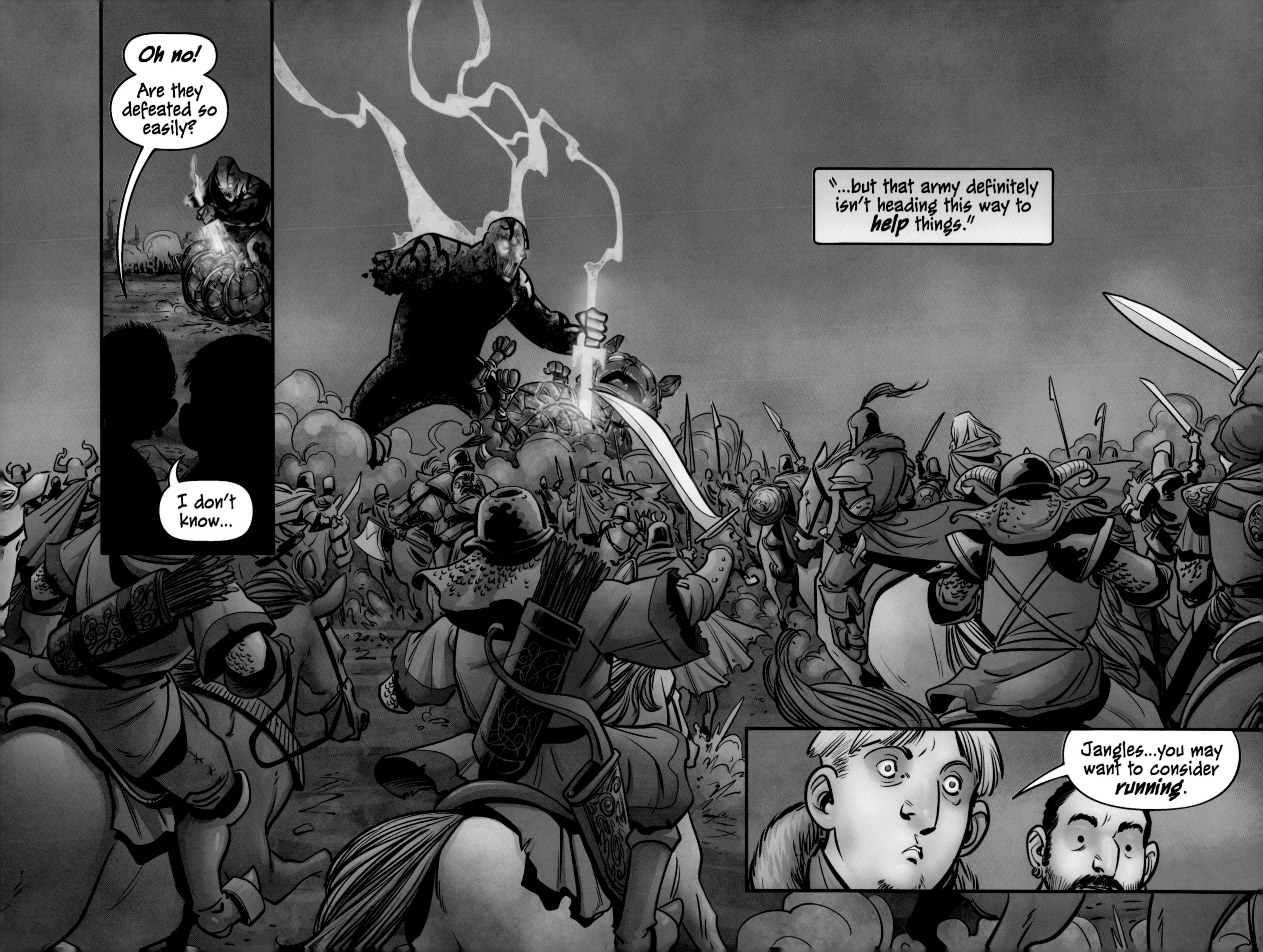
Oh no!
Are they defeated so easily?
I don't know...
"...but that army definitely isn't heading this way to *help* things."
Jangles...you may want to consider *running*.

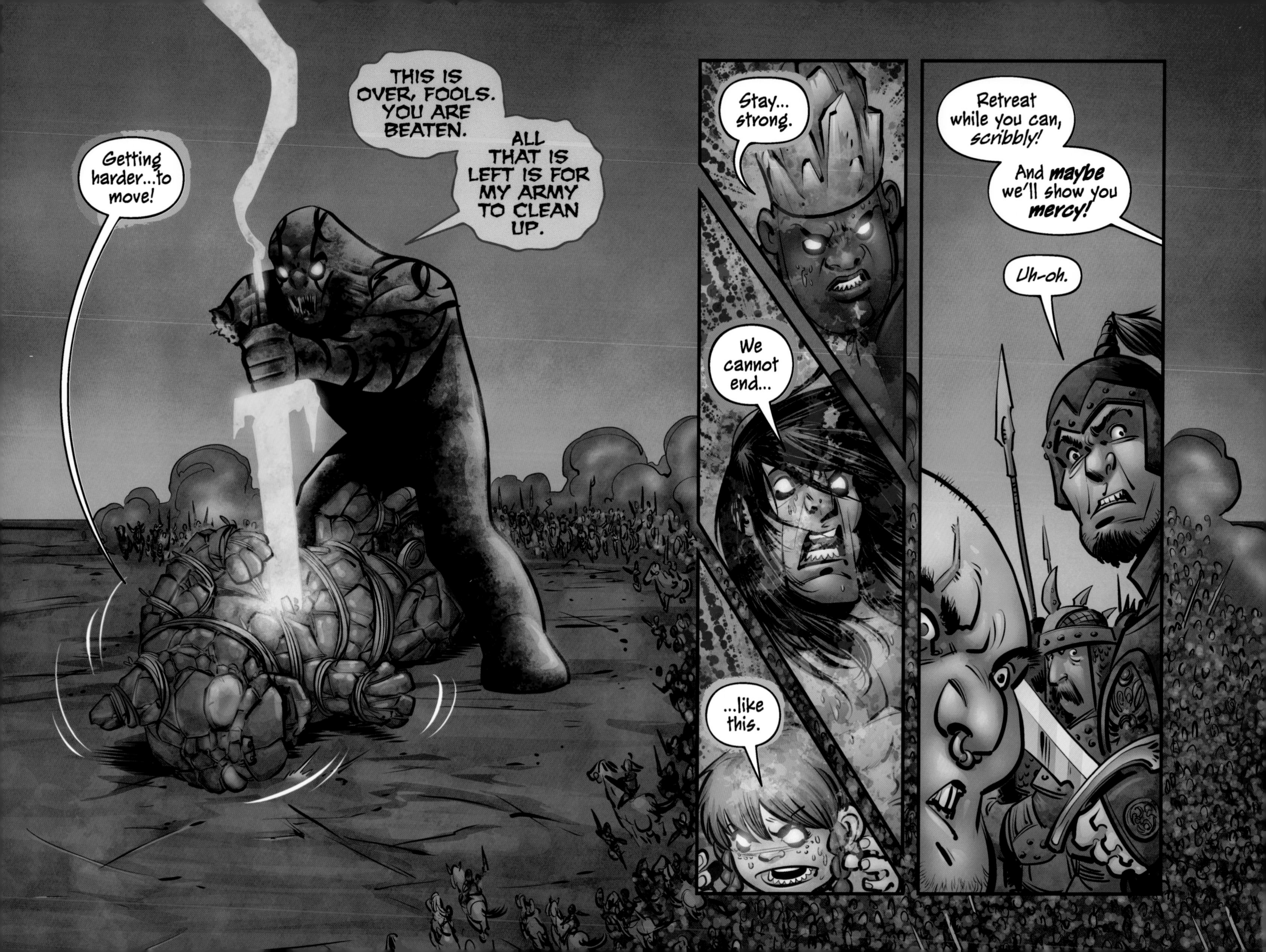
THIS IS OVER, FOOLS. YOU ARE BEATEN.
ALL THAT IS LEFT IS FOR MY ARMY TO CLEAN UP.
Getting harder...to move!
Stay... strong.
We cannot end...
...like this.
Retreat while you can, scribbly!
And **maybe** we'll show you **mercy!**
Uh-oh.

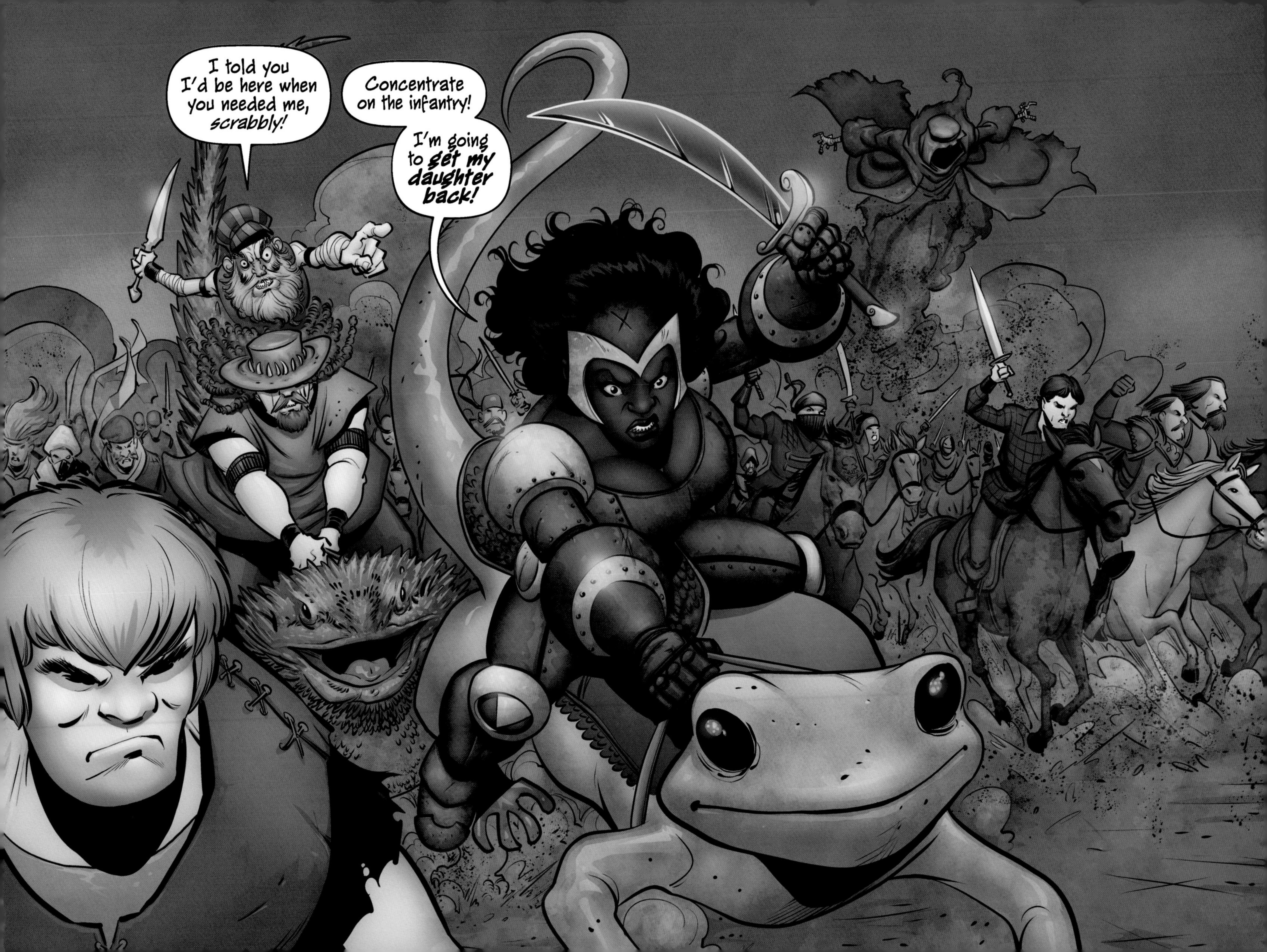
I told you I'd be here when you needed me, *scrabbly!*
Concentrate on the infantry!
I'm going to **get my daughter back!**

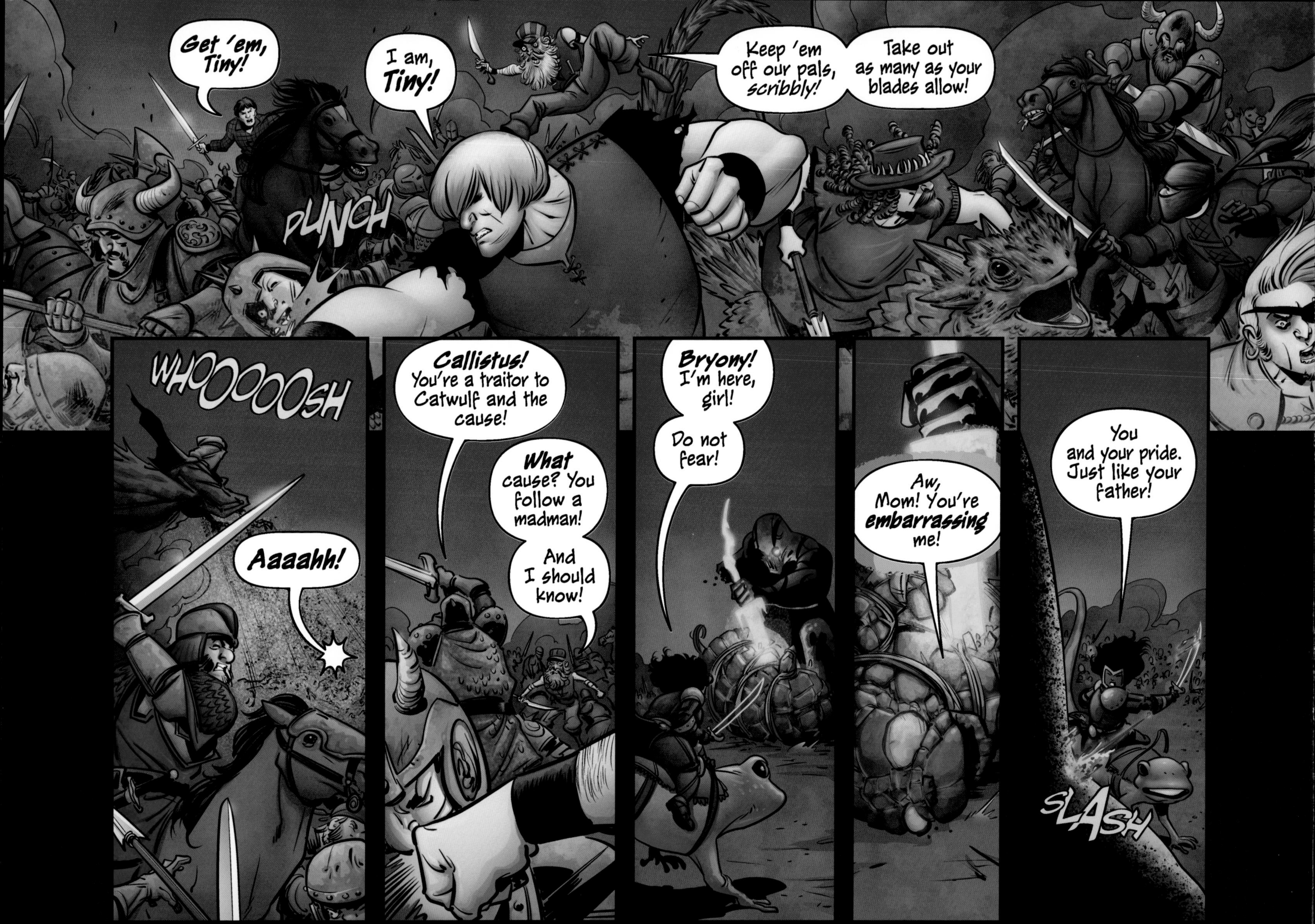
Get 'em, Tiny!
I am, Tiny!
PUNCH
Keep 'em off our pals, scribbly!
Take out as many as your blades allow!
WHOOOOOOSH
Aaaahh!
Callistus! You're a traitor to Catwulf and the cause!
What cause? You follow a madman!
And I should know!
Bryony! I'm here, girl!
Do not fear!
Aw, Mom! You're embarrassing me!
You and your pride. Just like your father!
SLASH

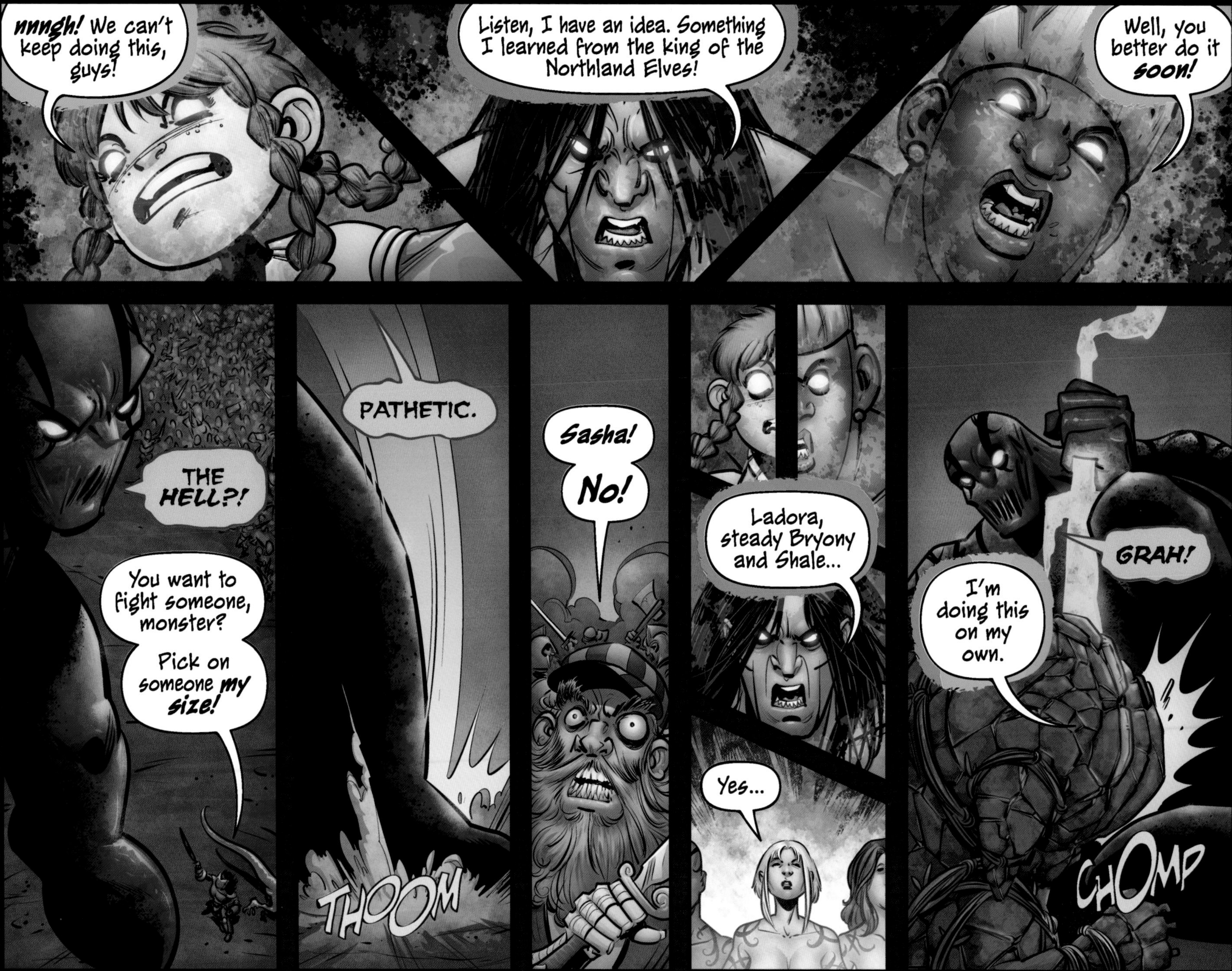
nnngh! We can't keep doing this, guys!
Listen, I have an idea. Something I learned from the king of the Northland Elves!
Well, you better do it soon!
THE HELL?!
You want to fight someone, monster?
Pick on someone my size!
PATHETIC.
THOOM
Sasha!
No!
Ladora, steady Bryony and Shale...
Yes...
GRAH!
I'm doing this on my own.
CHOMP

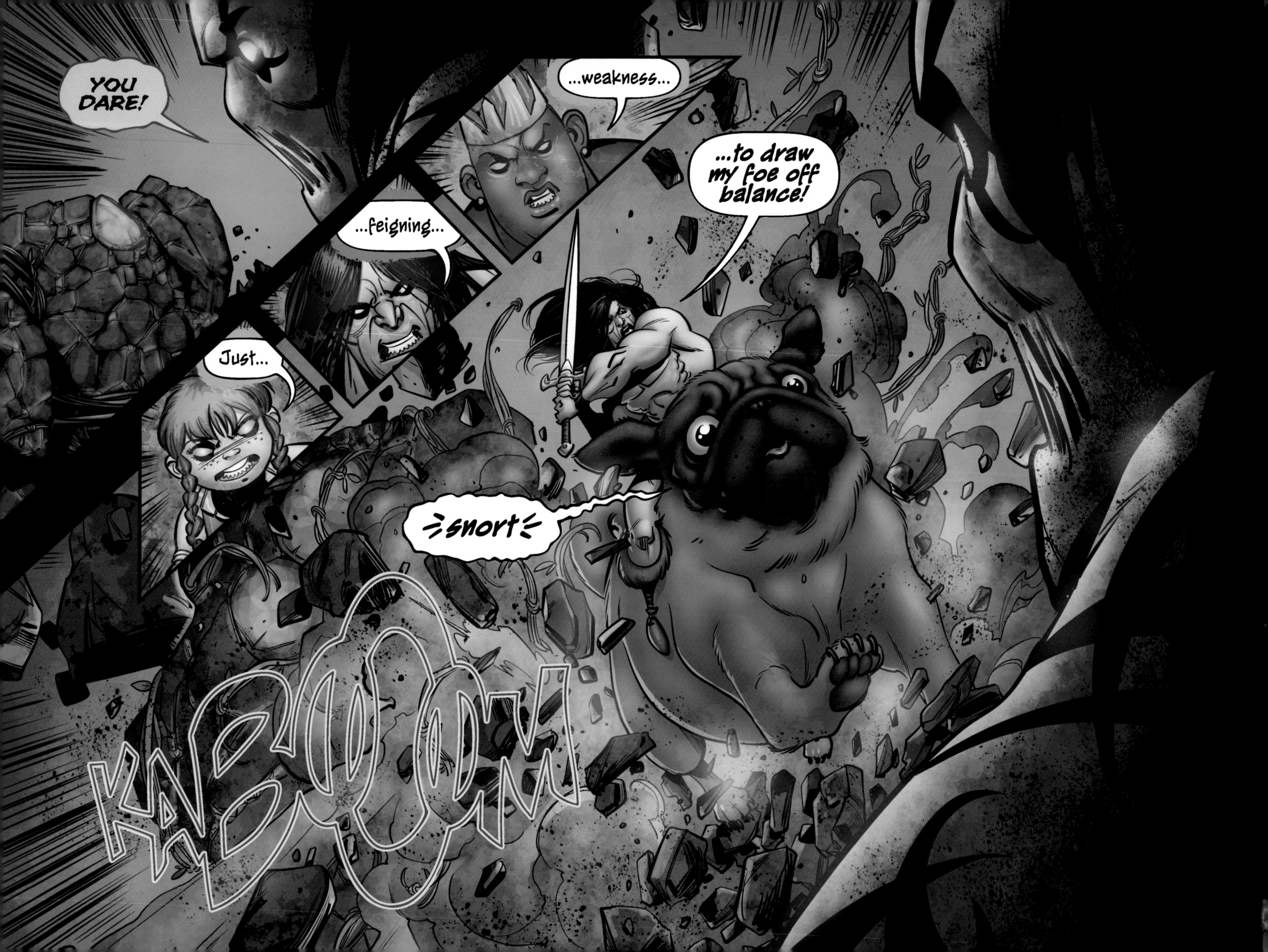
YOU DARE!
Just...
...feigning...
...weakness...
...to draw my foe off balance!
snort
KABOOOM

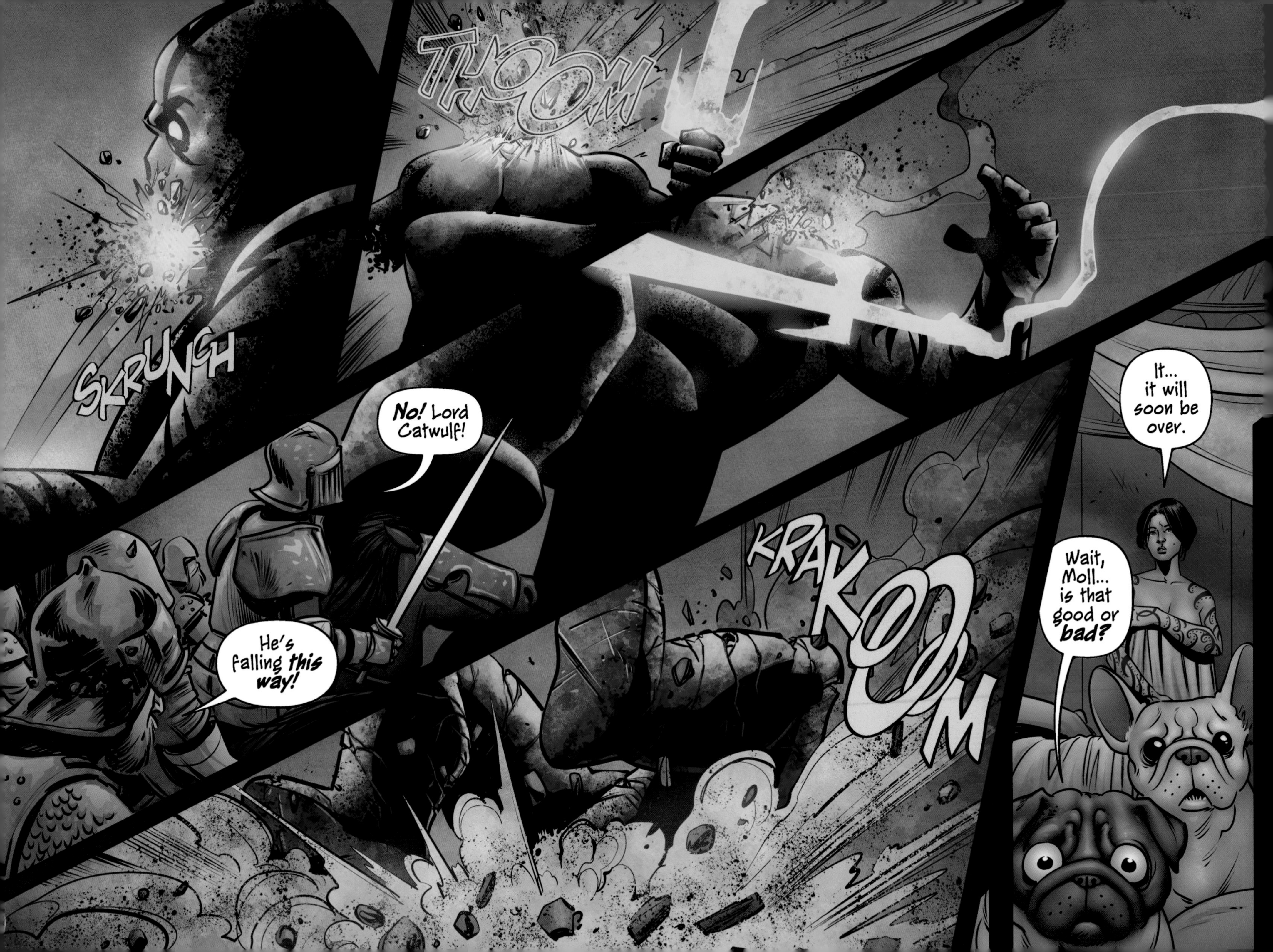
THOOM
SKRUNCH
No! Lord Catwulf!
He's falling this way!
KRAKOOOOM
It... it will soon be over.
Wait, Moll... is that good or bad?

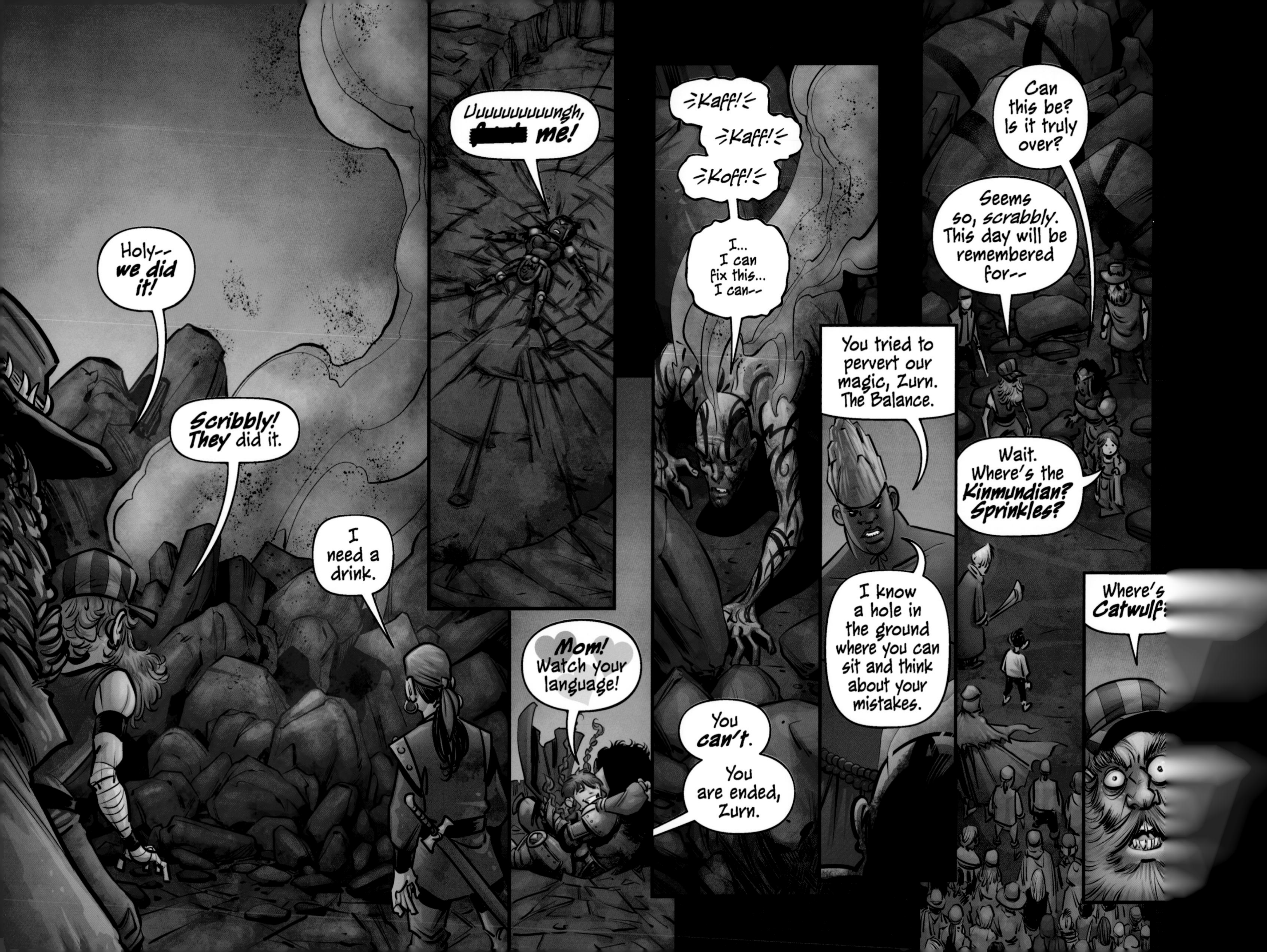

Holy-- we did it!
Scribbly! They did it.
I need a drink.
Uuuuuuuuuungh, [redacted] me!
Mom! Watch your language!
Kaff!
Kaff!
Koff!
I... I can fix this... I can--
You can't.
You are ended, Zurn.
You tried to pervert our magic, Zurn. The Balance.
I know a hole in the ground where you can sit and think about your mistakes.
Can this be? Is it truly over?
Seems so, scrabbly. This day will be remembered for--
Wait. Where's the Kinmundian? Sprinkles?
Where's Catwulf

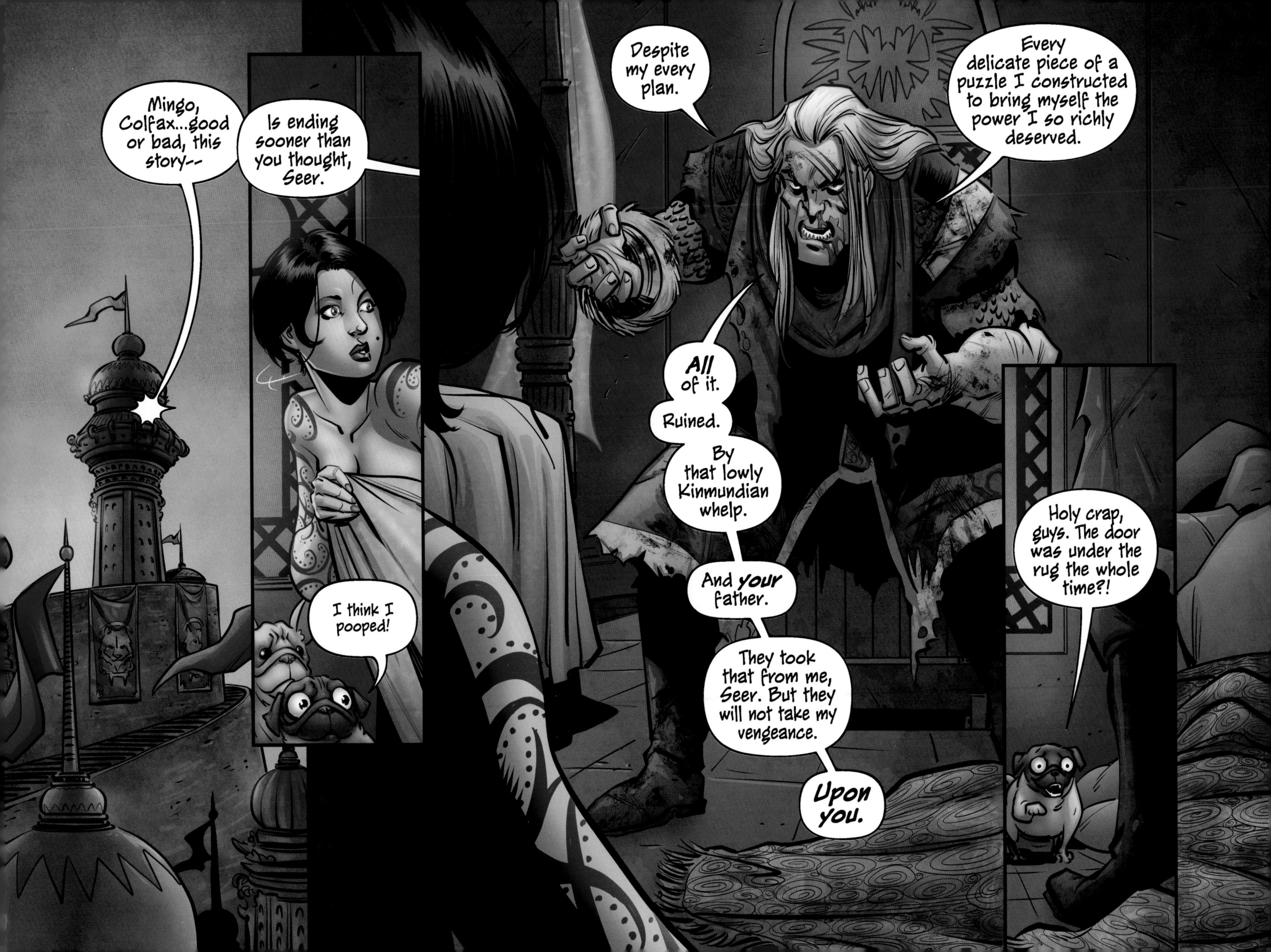
Mingo, Colfax...good or bad, this story--
Is ending sooner than you thought, Seer.
I think I pooped!
Despite my every plan.
Every delicate piece of a puzzle I constructed to bring myself the power I so richly deserved.
All of it.
Ruined.
By that lowly Kinmundian whelp.
And your father.
They took that from me, Seer. But they will not take my vengeance.
Upon you.
Holy crap, guys. The door was under the rug the whole time?!

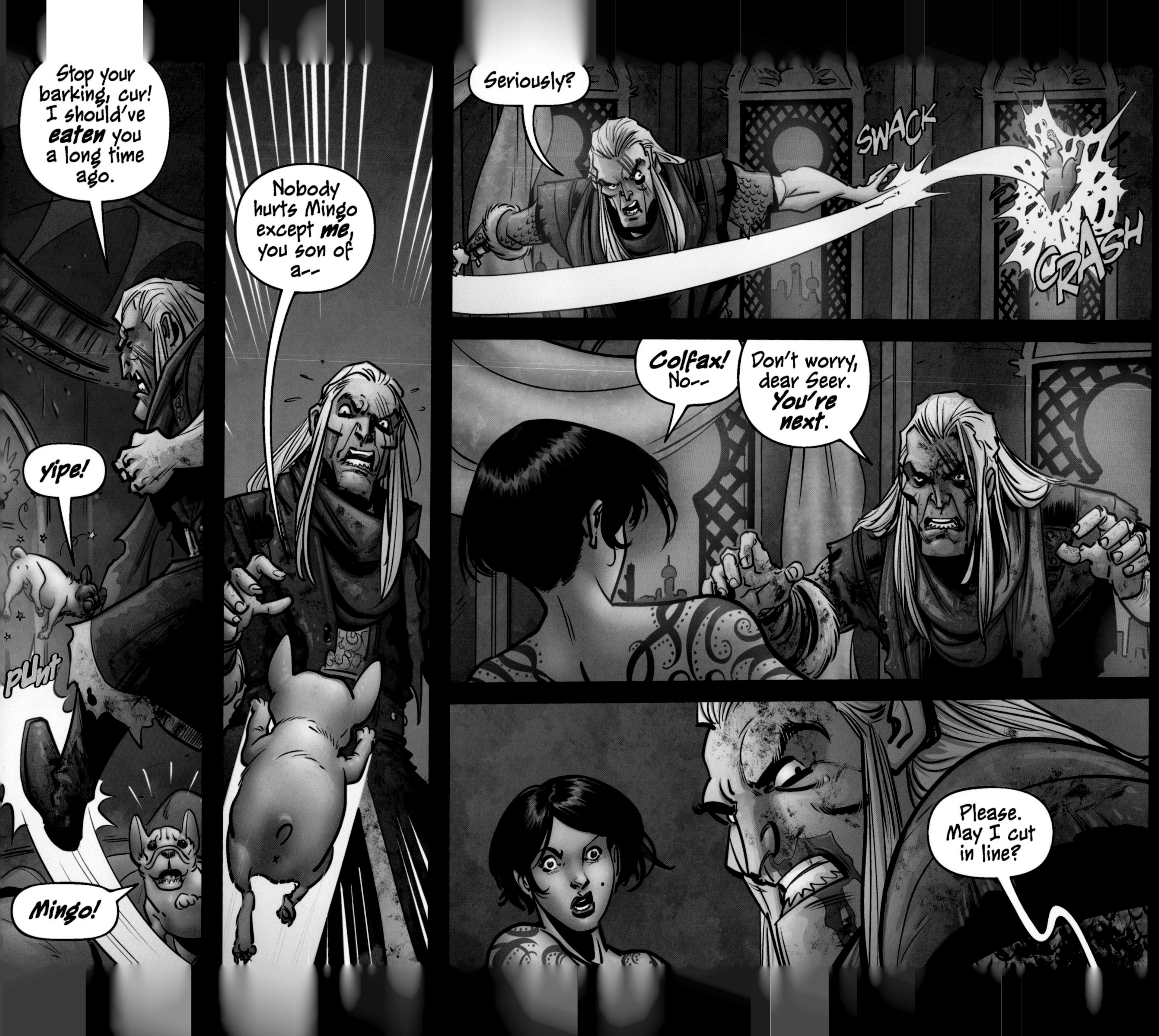

Stop your barking, cur! I should've *eaten* you a long time ago.
yipe!
pUnt
Mingo!
Nobody hurts Mingo except *me*, you son of a--
Seriously?
SWACK
CRASH
Colfax! No--
Don't worry, dear Seer. *You're next*.
Please. May I cut in line?

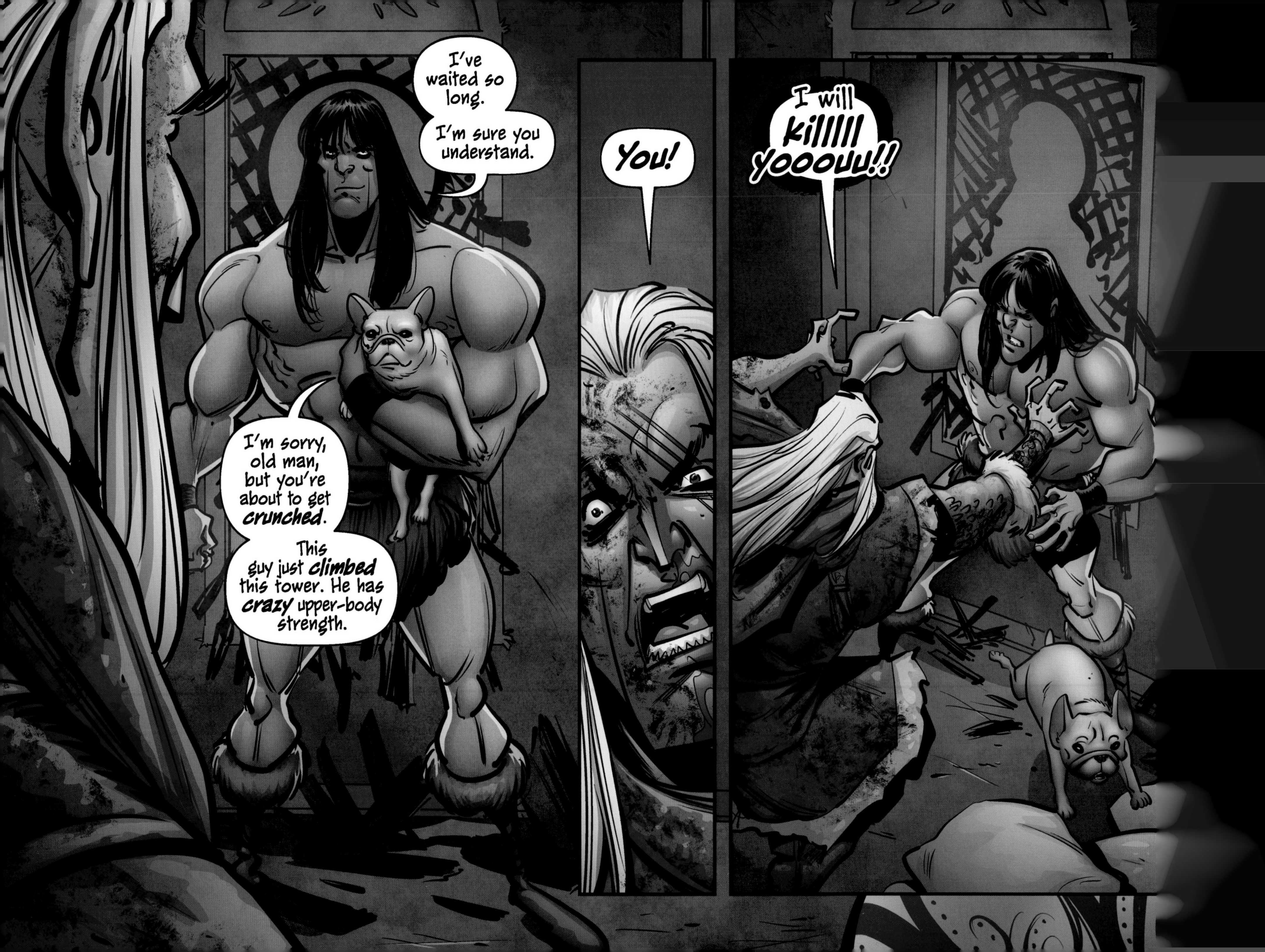

I've waited so long.
I'm sure you understand.
I'm sorry, old man, but you're about to get **crunched**.
This guy just **climbed** this tower. He has **crazy** upper-body strength.
You!
I will killlll yoooouu!!

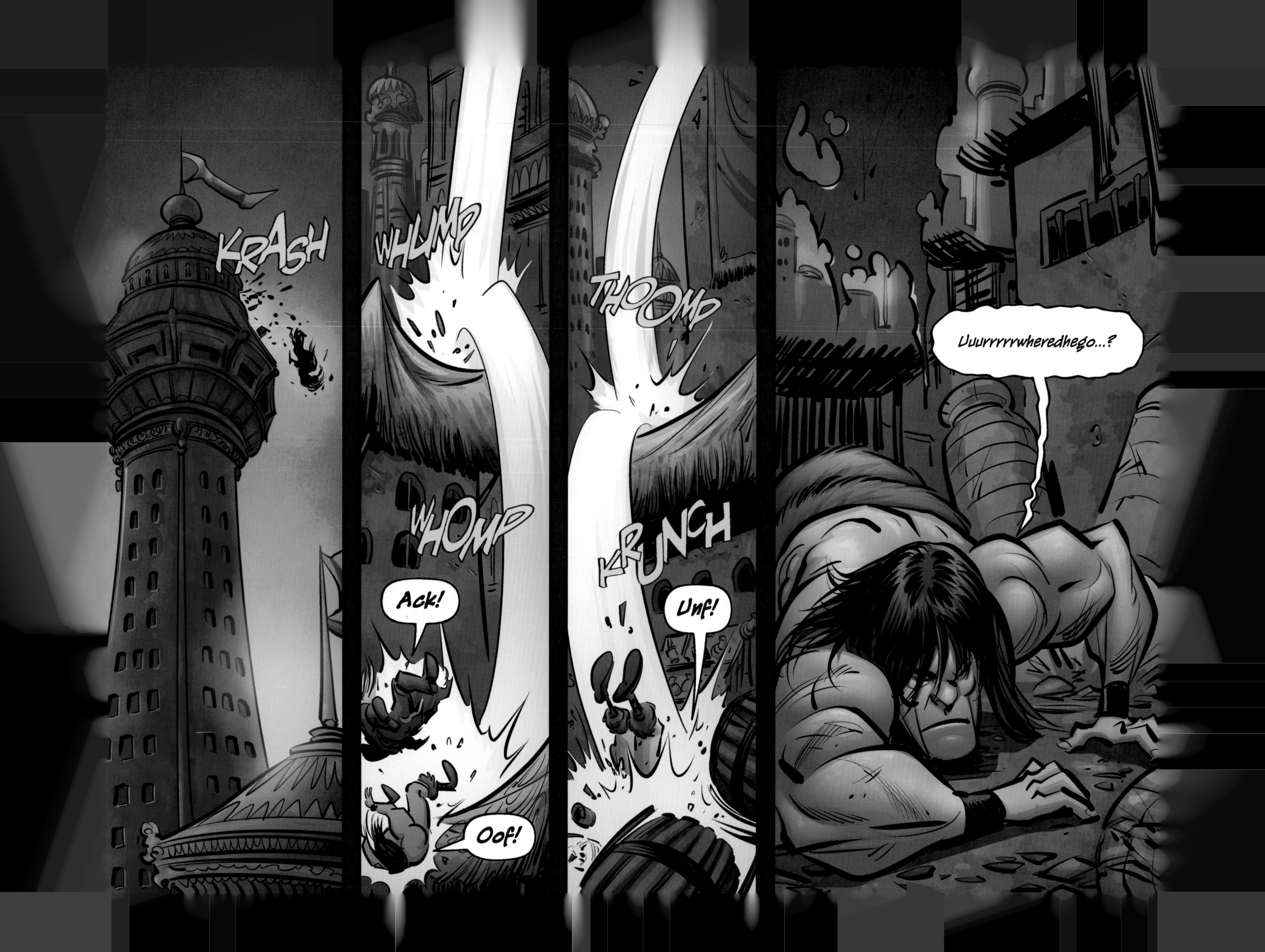

KRASH
WHUMP
WHOMP
Ack!
Oof!
THOOMP
KRUNCH
Unf!
Uuurrrrrwheredhego...?

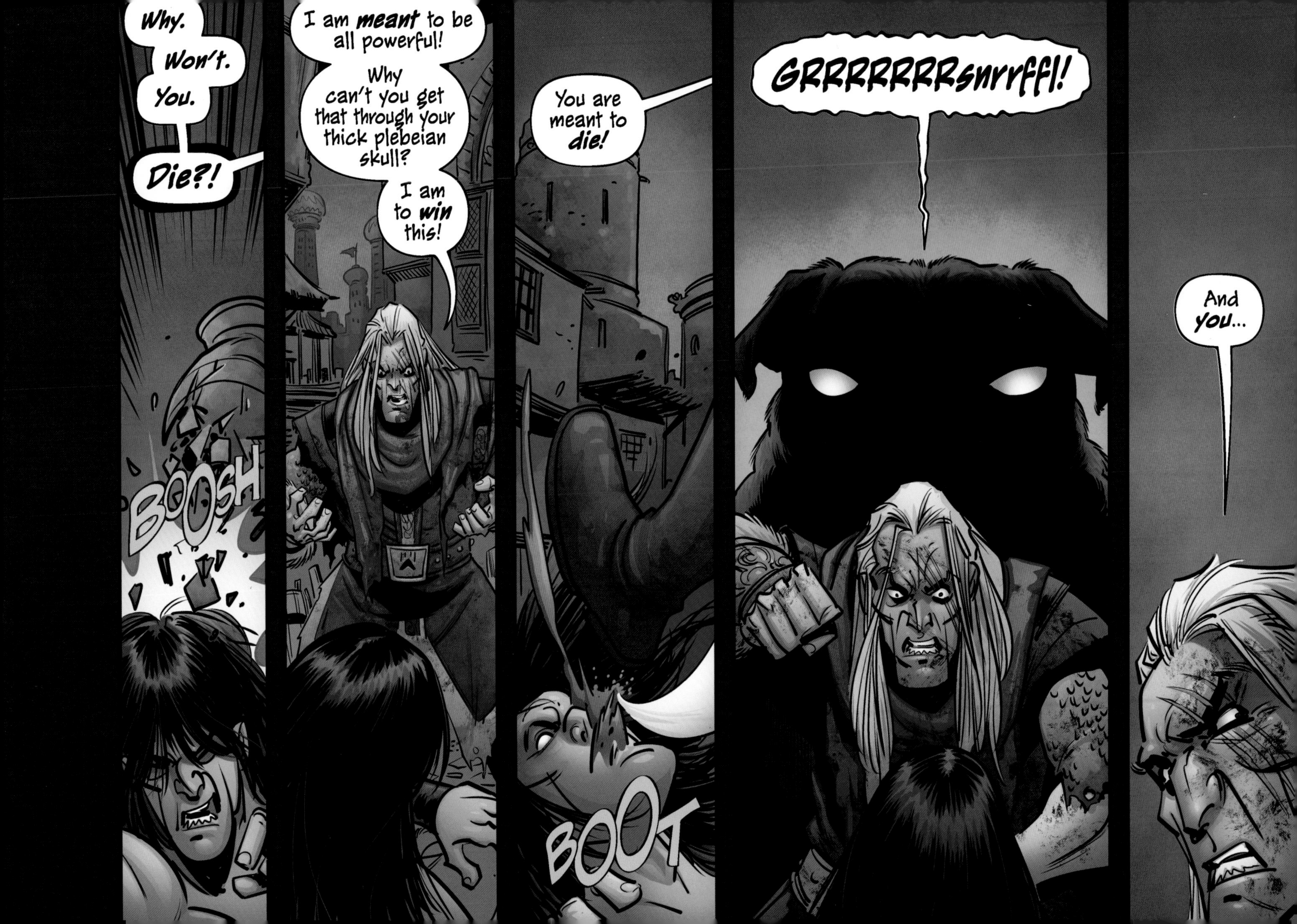
Why.
Won't.
You.
Die?!
BOOSH
I am meant to be all powerful!
Why can't you get that through your thick plebeian skull?
I am to win this!
You are meant to die!
BOOT
GRRRRRRRsnrrffl!
And you...

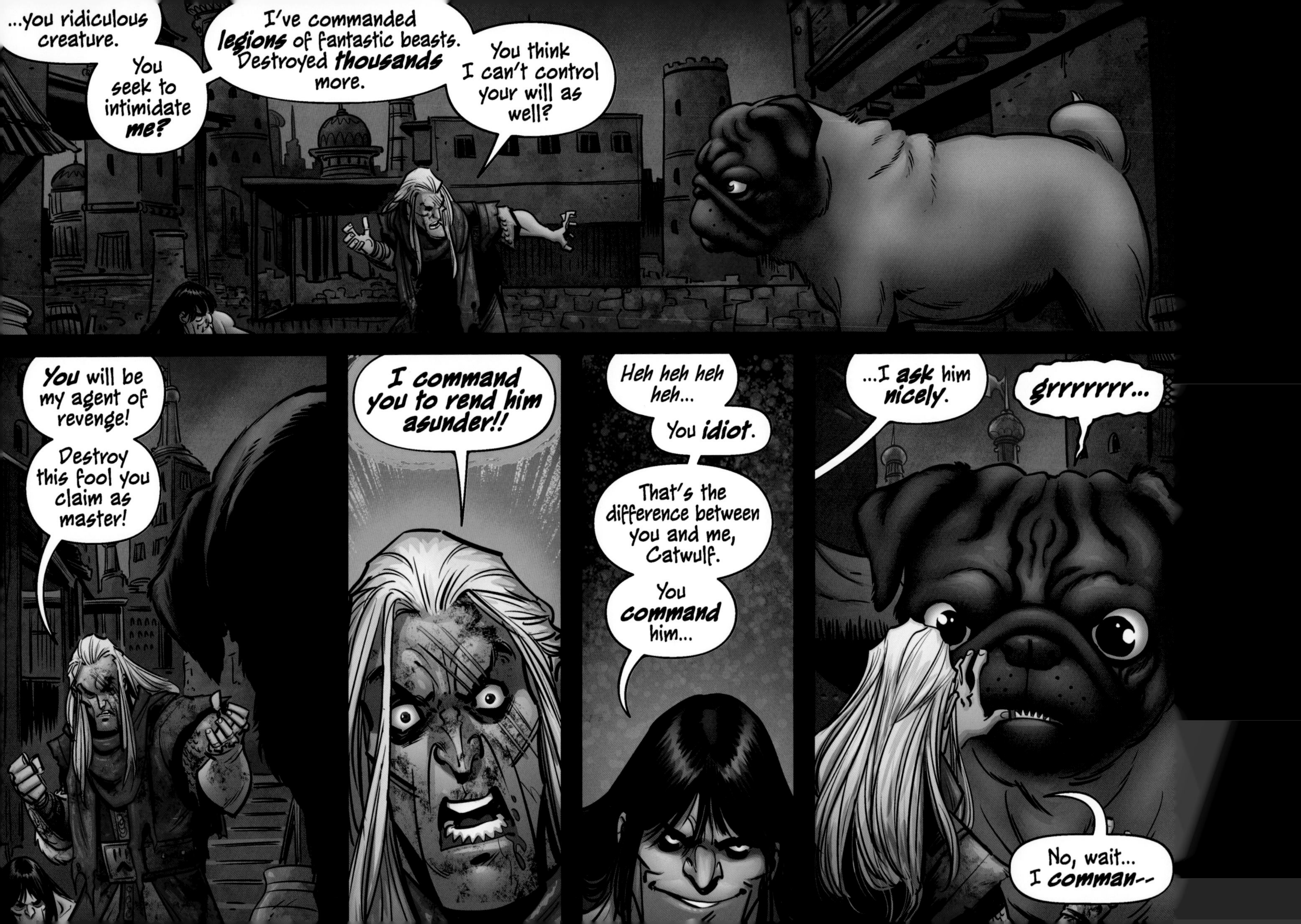
...you ridiculous creature.
You seek to intimidate me?
I've commanded legions of fantastic beasts. Destroyed thousands more.
You think I can't control your will as well?
You will be my agent of revenge!
Destroy this fool you claim as master!
I command you to rend him asunder!!
Heh heh heh heh...
You idiot.
That's the difference between you and me, Catwulf.
You command him...
...I ask him nicely.
grrrrrrr...
No, wait... I comman--

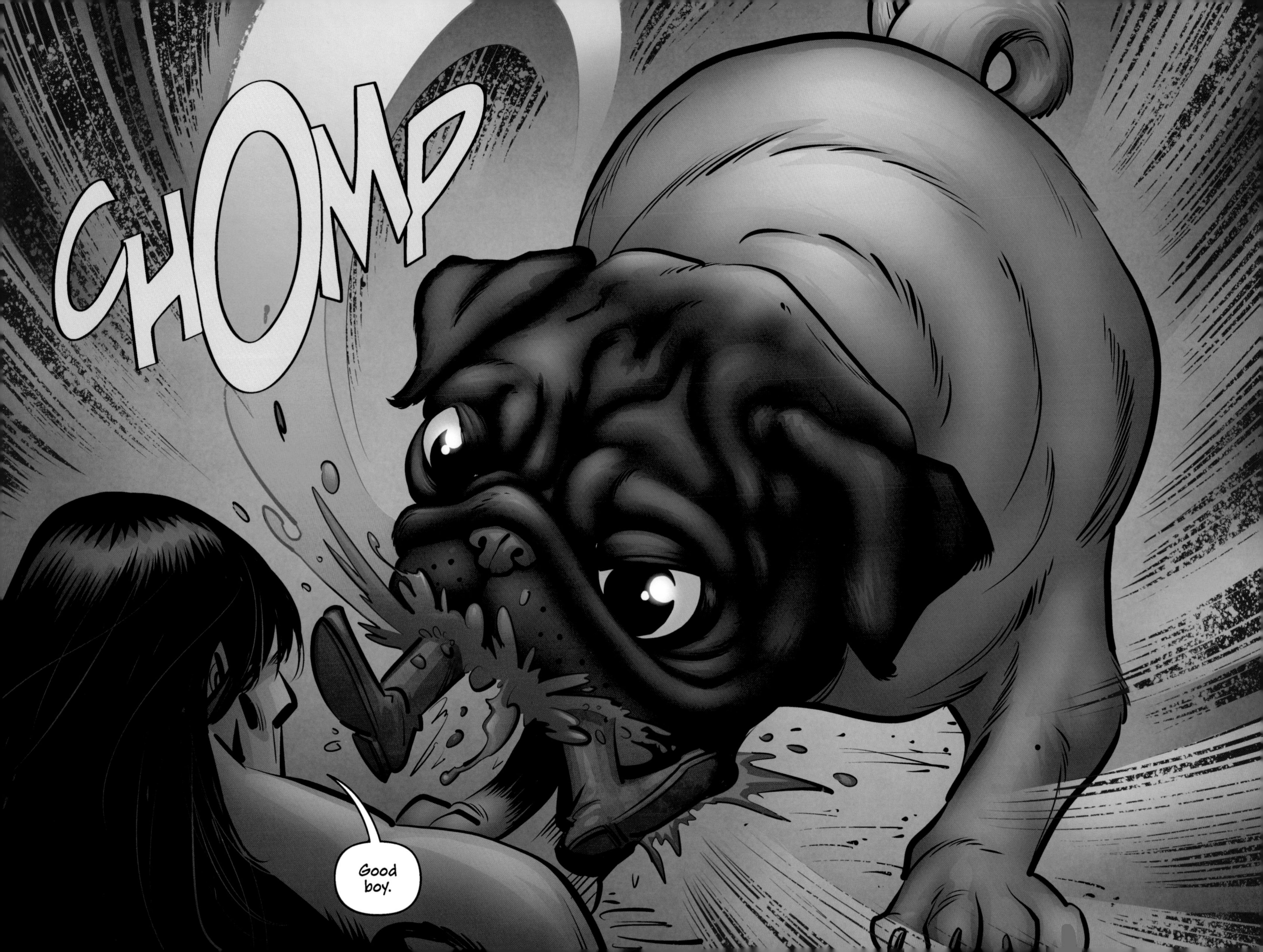
CHOMP
Good boy.

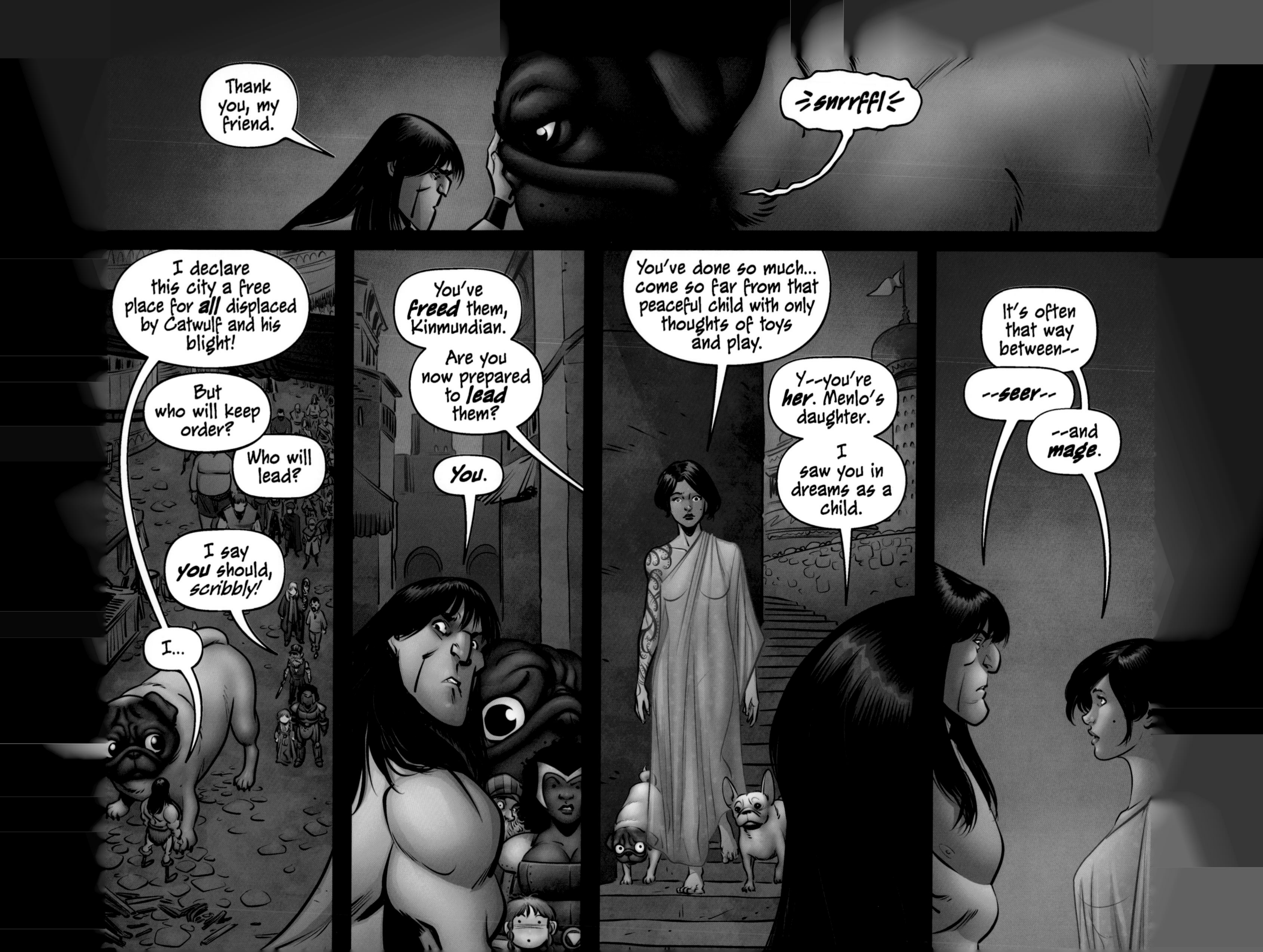
Thank you, my friend.
snrrffl
I declare this city a free place for all displaced by Catwulf and his blight!
But who will keep order?
Who will lead?
I say you should, scribbly!
I...
You've freed them, Kinmundian.
Are you now prepared to lead them?
You.
You've done so much... come so far from that peaceful child with only thoughts of toys and play.
Y--you're her. Menlo's daughter.
I saw you in dreams as a child.
It's often that way between--
--seer--
--and mage.

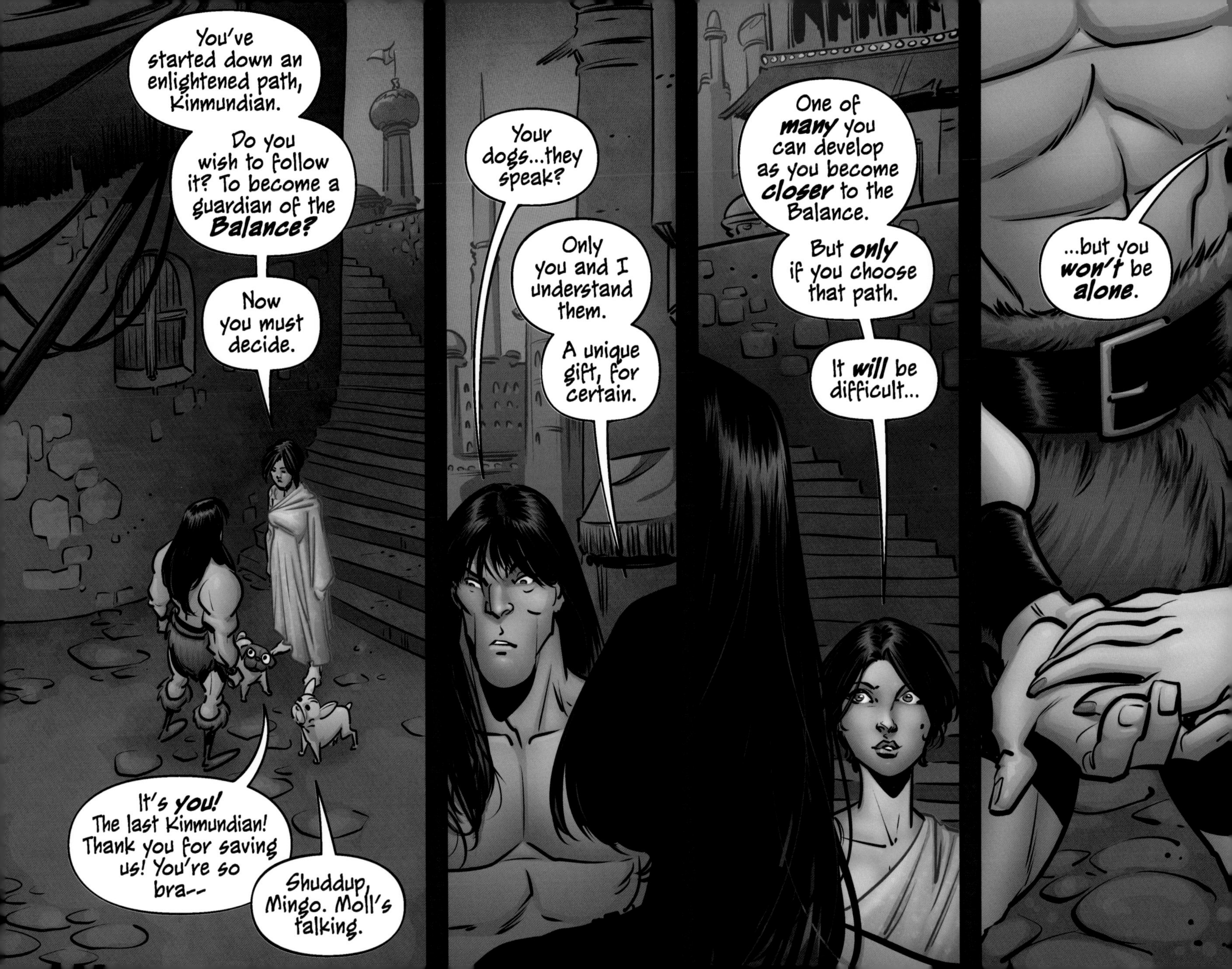
You've started down an enlightened path, Kinmundian.
Do you wish to follow it? To become a guardian of the *Balance?*
Now you must decide.
It's *you!* The last Kinmundian! Thank you for saving us! You're so bra--
Shuddup, Mingo. Moll's talking.
Your dogs...they speak?
Only you and I understand them.
A unique gift, for certain.
One of *many* you can develop as you become *closer* to the Balance.
But *only* if you choose that path.
It *will* be difficult...
...but you *won't* be *alone*.

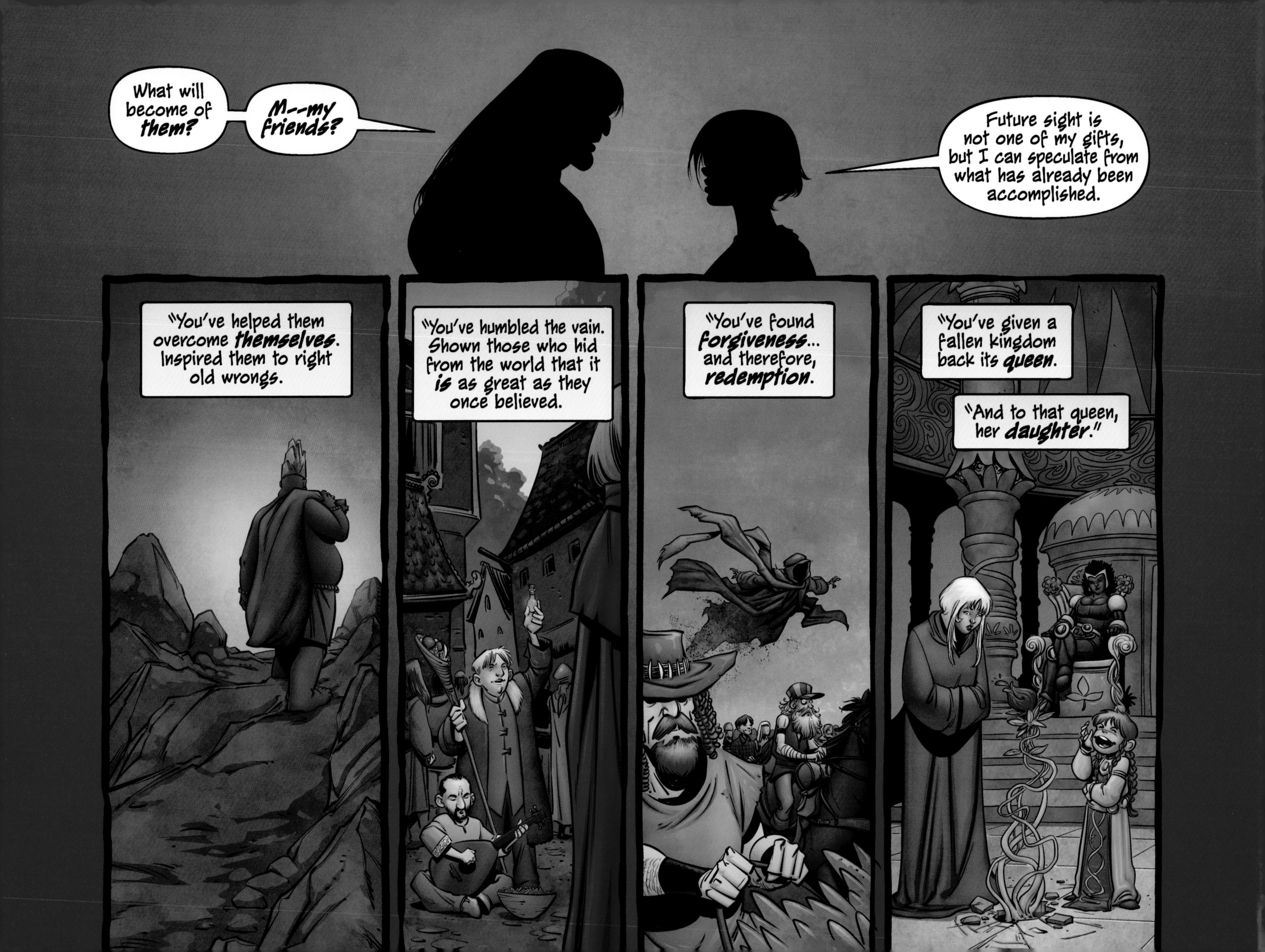
What will become of them?
M--my friends?
Future sight is not one of my gifts, but I can speculate from what has already been accomplished.
"You've helped them overcome themselves. Inspired them to right old wrongs.
"You've humbled the vain. Shown those who hid from the world that it is as great as they once believed.
"You've found forgiveness... and therefore, redemption.
"You've given a fallen kingdom back its queen.
"And to that queen, her daughter."

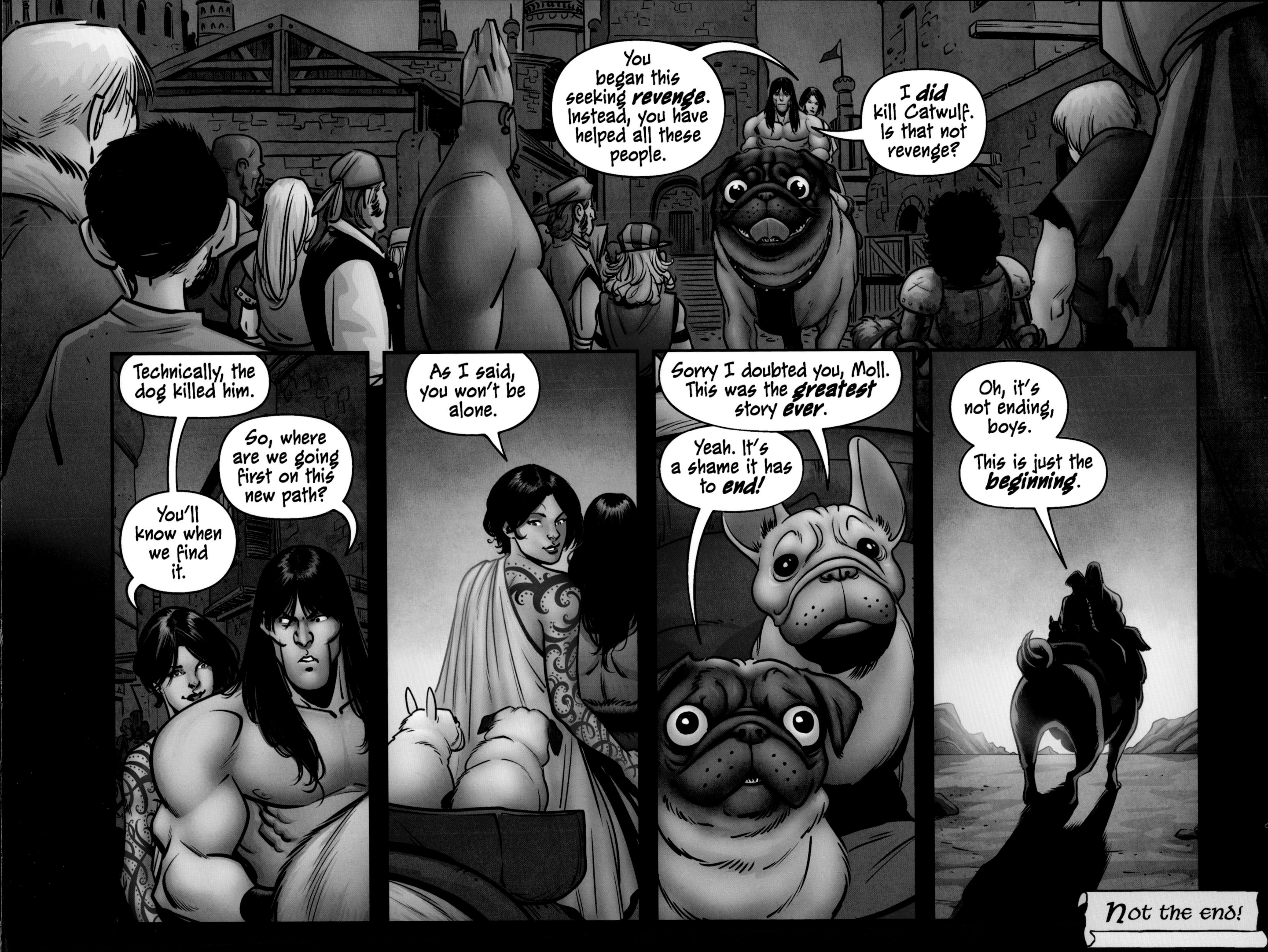

You began this seeking revenge. Instead, you have helped all these people.
I did kill Catwulf. Is that not revenge?
Technically, the dog killed him.
So, where are we going first on this new path?
You'll know when we find it.
As I said, you won't be alone.
Sorry I doubted you, Moll. This was the greatest story ever.
Yeah. It's a shame it has to end!
Oh, it's not ending, boys.
This is just the beginning.
Not the end!

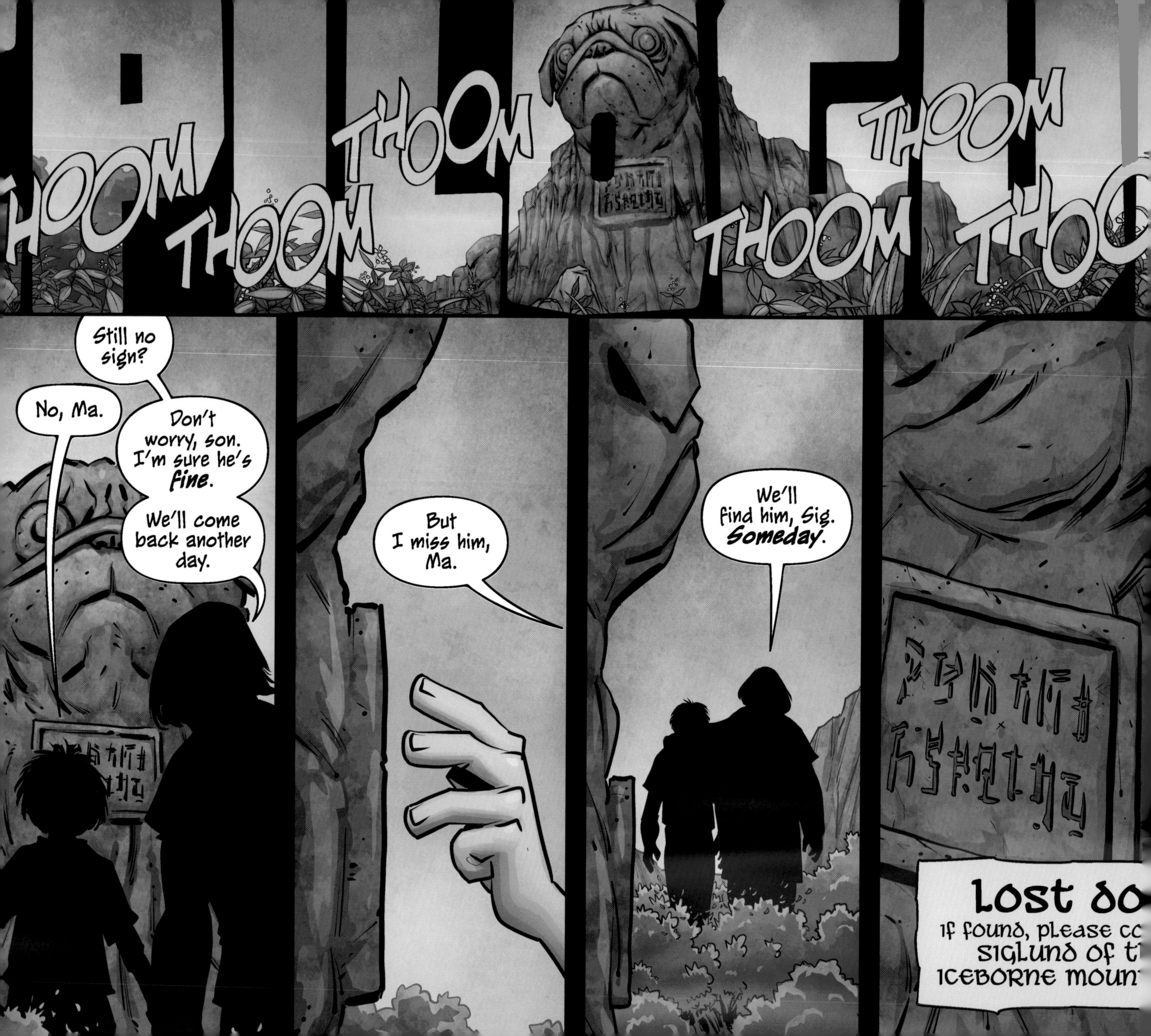
THOOM
THOOM
THOOM
THOOM
THOOM
Still no sign?
No, Ma.
Don't worry, son. I'm sure he's *fine*.
We'll come back another day.
But I miss him, Ma.
We'll find him, Sig. **Someday**.
LOST DO
IF FOUND, PLEASE CO
SIGLUND OF T
ICEBORNE MOUNT

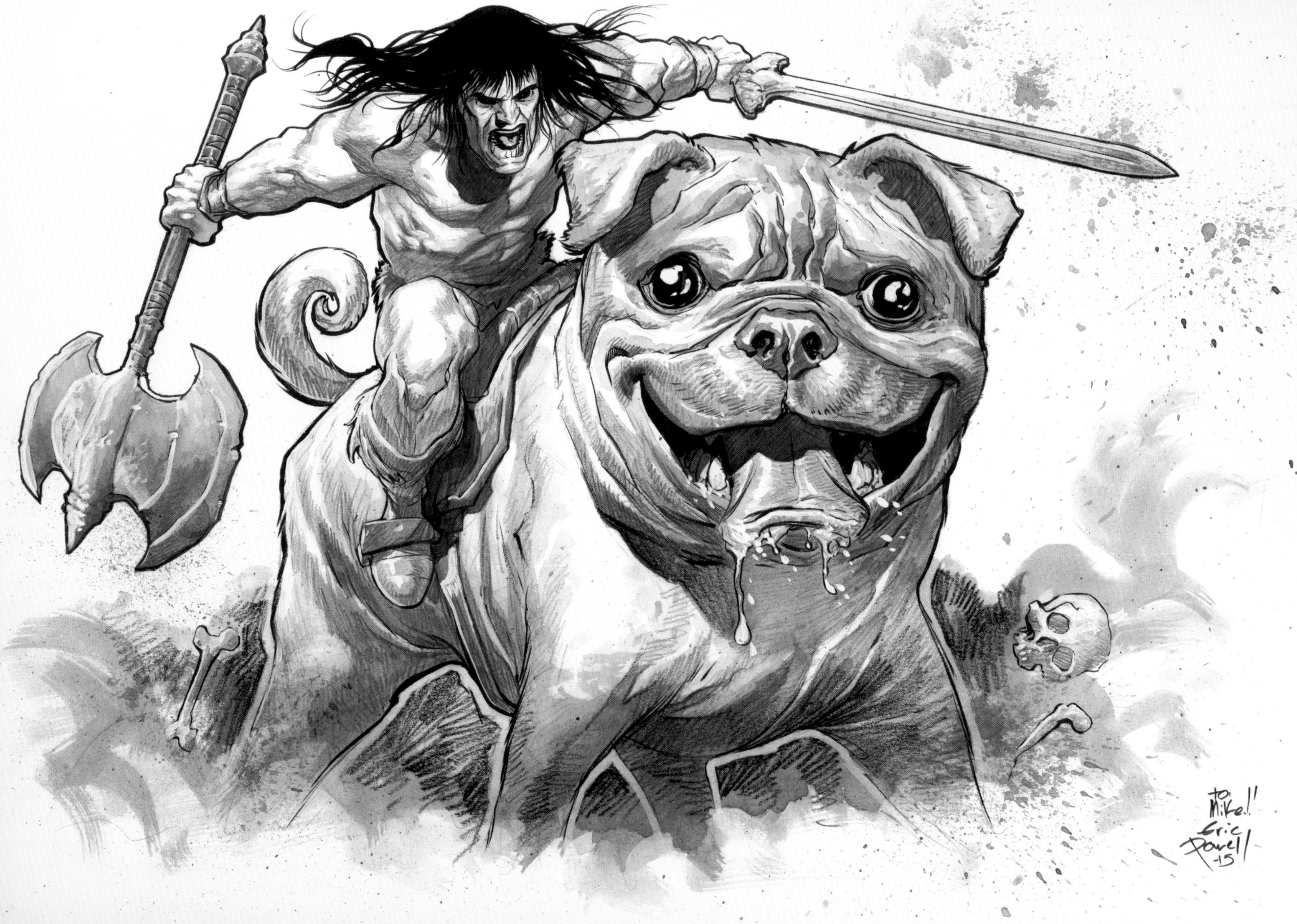
to Mike!!
Eric Powell
-15

Eric Powell

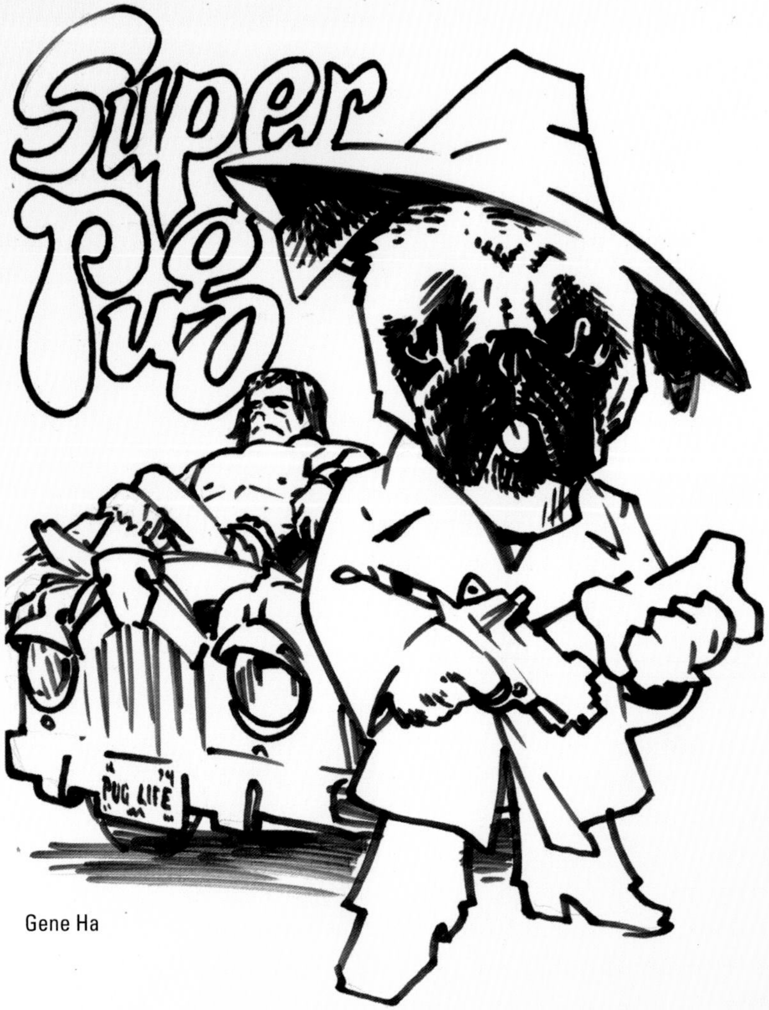
Super Pug
PUG LIFE

Gene Ha

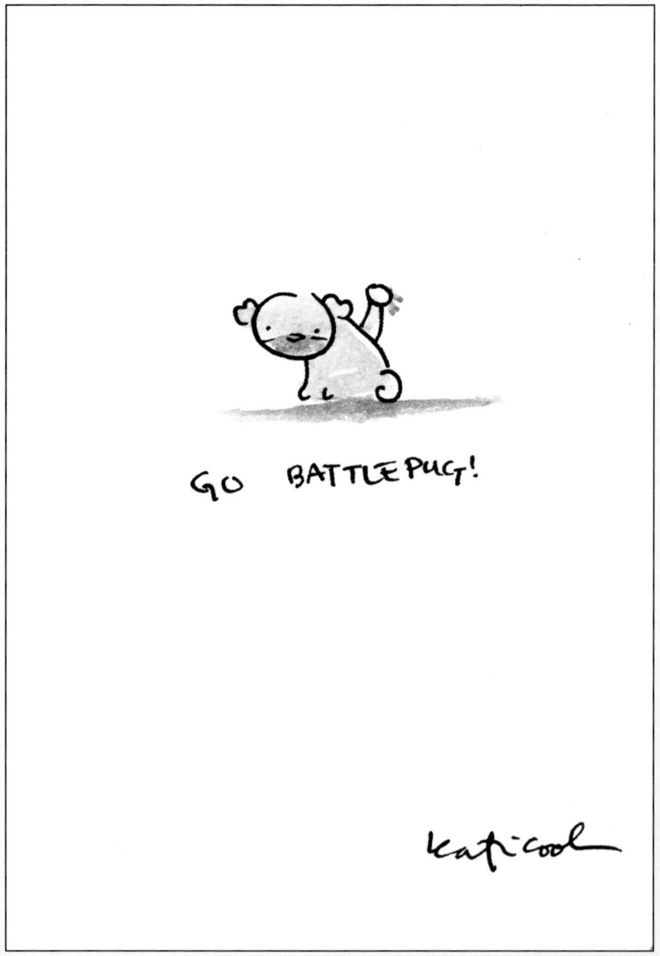
GO BATTLEPUG!
katiecook

Katie Cook

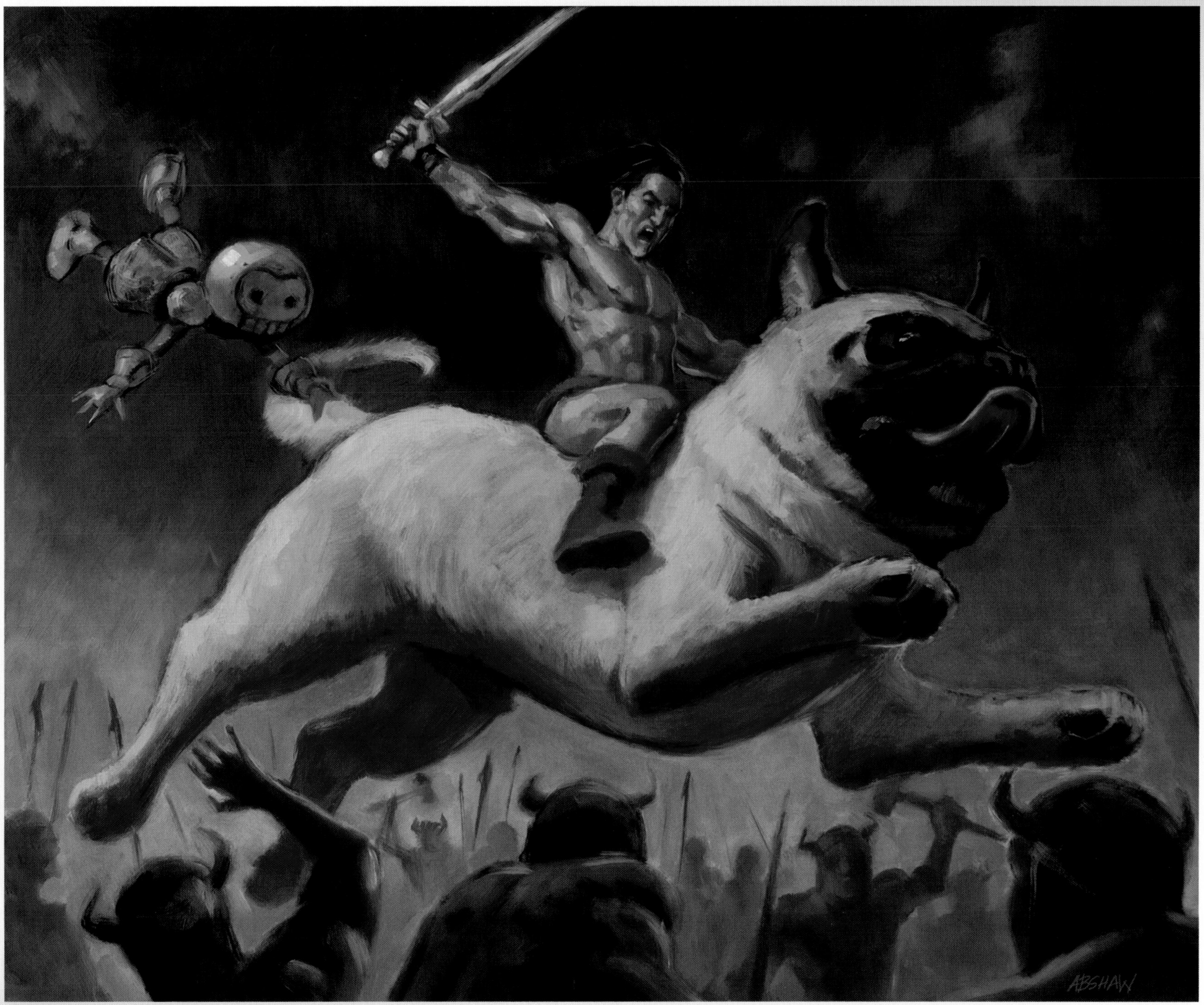
ABSHAW

Adam Shaw

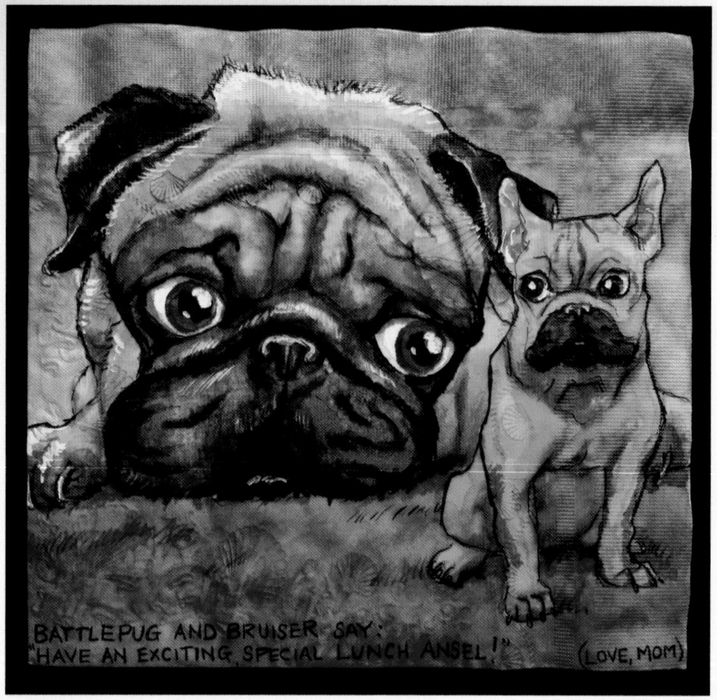
BATTLEPUG AND BRUISER SAY:
"HAVE AN EXCITING, SPECIAL LUNCH ANSEL!"
(LOVE, MOM)

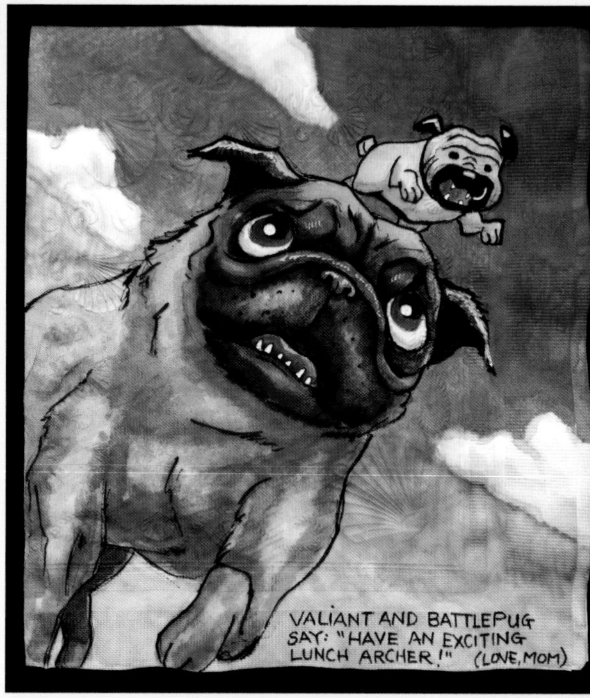
VALIANT AND BATTLEPUG
SAY: "HAVE AN EXCITING
LUNCH ARCHER!" (LOVE, MOM)

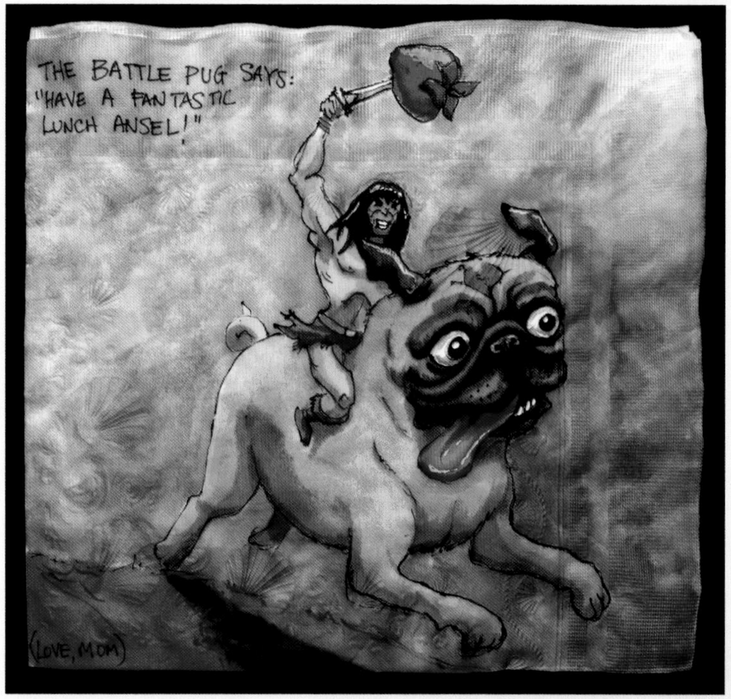
THE BATTLE PUG SAYS:
"HAVE A FANTASTIC
LUNCH ANSEL!"
(LOVE, MOM)

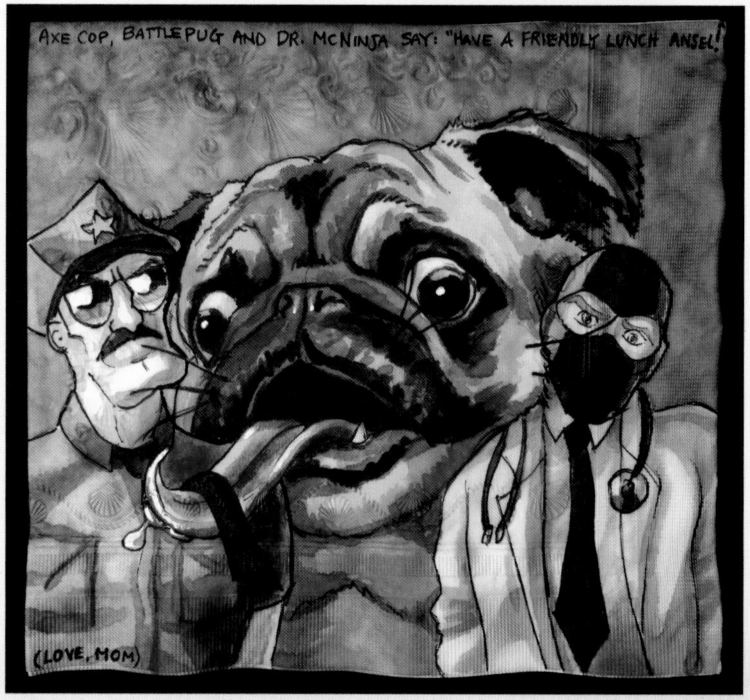
AXE COP, BATTLEPUG AND DR. MCNINJA SAY: "HAVE A FRIENDLY LUNCH ANSEL!"
(LOVE, MOM)

Nina Levy

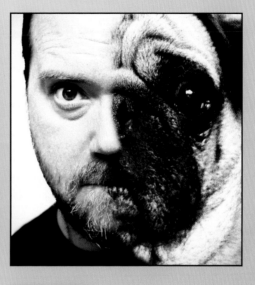

MIKE NORTON

Mike Norton has many years of Marvel and DC credits and is currently the creator of the Harvey and Eisner Award–winning webcomic *Battlepug*. He created the Dark Horse Comics series *The Answer!* and cocreated the critically acclaimed Image Comics series *Revival* with studiomate Tim Seeley. He lives in Chicago with his wife and pugs. He is also very, very tall.

ALLEN PASSALAQUA

Allen is a professional comic color artist, as well as being involved in promoting culture and art and bringing together the creative community. Combining traditional and pop-culture influences, Allen has been commissioned to create artwork for several national parks, the San Diego Zoo, and the Grand Canyon, has storyboarded Emmy-winning commercials, and has worked on various mass-media-outlet projects. His coloring work includes *Justice Society of America*, *Spider-Man*, *Green Arrow/Black Canary*, *Detective Comics*, and many others. He is not as tall as Mike.

CHRIS CRANK

The letterer, musician, and editing pal Crank is believed to be a myth, and he must let the world think that he is a myth, until he can find a way to control the snotty spirit that dwells within him. Crank once babysat Mike's first pug for a whole weekend without damaging him, and he has a podcast with Mike at CrankCast.net.

DARK HORSE BRINGS YOU THE BEST IN WEBCOMICS!

COLLECT ALL OF YOUR FAVORITE ONLINE SENSATIONS, NOW IN PRINT WITH LOADS OF AWESOME EXTRAS NOT FOUND ANYWHERE ELSE!

ACHEWOOD
By Chris Onstad

Since 2001, cult comic favorite *Achewood* has built a six-figure international following. Intelligent, hilarious, and adult but not filthy, it's the strip you'll wish you'd discovered as an underappreciated fifteen-year-old. "I'm addicted to *Achewood*. Chris Onstad is a dark, hilarious genius." –Dave Barry

Volume 1: The Great Outdoor Fight HC
ISBN 978-1-59307-997-0 | $14.99

Volume 2: Worst Song, Played on Ugliest Guitar HC
ISBN 978-1-59582-239-0 | $15.99

Volume 3: A Home for Scared People HC
ISBN 978-1-59582-450-9 | $16.99

AXE COP
By Malachai Nicolle and Ethan Nicolle

Created by five-year-old Malachai Nicolle and illustrated by his older brother, the cartoonist Ethan Nicolle, these *Axe Cop* volumes collect the hit webcomic that has captured the world's attention with its insanely imaginative adventures, as well as the *Axe Cop* print-only adventures. Whether he's fighting gun-toting dinosaurs, teaming up with Ninja Moon Warriors, or answering readers' questions via his insightful advice column, "Ask Axe Cop," the adventures of Axe Cop and his incomparable team of crime fighters will delight and perplex even the most stoic of readers.

Volume 1
ISBN 978-1-59582-681-7 | $14.99

Volume 2: Bad Guy Earth
ISBN 978-1-59582-825-5 | $12.99

Volume 3
ISBN 978-1-59582-911-5 | $14.99

Volume 4: President of the World
ISBN 978-1-61655-057-8 | $12.99

BATTLEPUG
By Mike Norton, Allen Passalaqua, and Crank

The epic tale of blood and drool! Join Moll, and her dogs Mingo and Colfax, as she recounts the legend of the fearless barbarian and his freakishly large pug.

Volume 1: Blood and Drool
ISBN 978-1-59582-972-6 | $14.99

Volume 2: This Savage Bone
ISBN 978-1-61655-201-5 | $14.99

Volume 3: Sit. Stay. Die!
ISBN 978-1-61655-594-8 | $14.99

Volume 4: The Devil's Biscuit
ISBN 978-1-61655-864-2 | $14.99

PENNY ARCADE
By Jerry Holkins and Mike Krahulik

Penny Arcade, the comic strip for gamers, by gamers, is now available in comic shops and bookstores everywhere. Experience the joy of being a hardcore gamer as expressed in hilariously witty vignettes of random vulgarity and mindless violence!

Volume 1: Attack of the Bacon Robots! TPB
ISBN 978-1-59307-444-9 | $12.99

Volume 2: Epic Legends of the Magic Sword Kings TPB
ISBN 978-1-59307-541-5 | $12.99

Volume 3: The WarSun Prophecies TPB
ISBN 978-1-59307-635-1 | $12.99

Volume 4: Birds Are Weird TPB
ISBN 978-1-59307-773-0 | $12.99

Volume 5: The Case of the Mummy's Gold TPB
ISBN 978-1-59307-814-0 | $12.99

THE ADVENTURES OF DR. MCNINJA
By Christopher Hastings

He's a doctor! He's a ninja! Read about his mighty exploits! These books offer a hefty dose of science, action, and outrageous comedy. With haunted spaceships, sentient dinosaurs, and an evil unicorn motorcycle, it's more adventure than your puny mind can handle!

Night Powers
ISBN 978-1-59582-709-8 | $19.99

Timefist
ISBN 978-1-61655-069-1 | $19.99

Omnibus
ISBN 978-1-61655-112-4 | $24.99

WONDERMARK
By David Malki

Dark Horse Comics is proud to present these handsome hardbound collections of David Malki's Ignatz-nominated comic strip *Wondermark*. Malki repurposes illustrations and engravings from nineteenth century books into hilarious, collage-style comic strips. More than just webcomic collections, the *Wondermark* books have been praised for their magnificent design and loads of extra content for casual readers and superfans alike.

Volume 1: Beards of Our Forefathers HC
ISBN 978-1-59307-984-0 | $14.99

Volume 2: Clever Tricks to Stave Off Death HC
ISBN 978-1-59582-329-8 | $14.99

Volume 3: Dapper Caps & Pedal-Copters HC
ISBN 978-1-59582-449-3 | $16.99

DARK HORSE BOOKS

DarkHorse.com

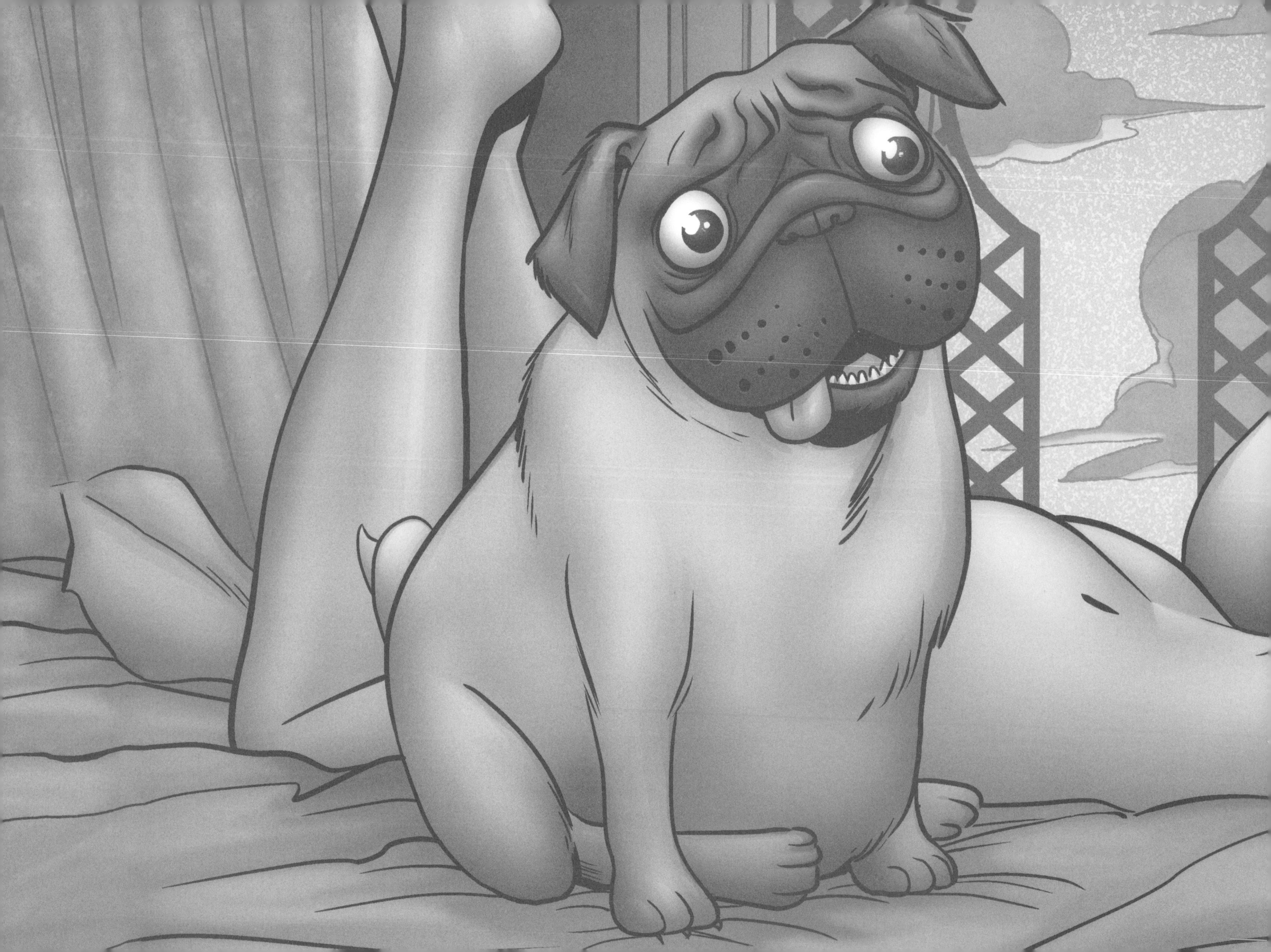